# Pearson's Canal Compa[nion]
## OXFORD & GRAND UN[ION]

CW00968097

Published by J.M.Pearson & Son Ltd, Tatenhill Common, Staffordshire DE13 9RS Tel/fax 01283 713674  www.jmpearson.co.uk
Copyright: J. M. Pearson - All rights reserved. Fourth edition revised 2000. ISBN 0 907864 80 5 Printed by Nexus & Lithomaster of Warwick

# tillerman

Technology is a two-edged sword. The opportunity is there to update the *Canal Companions* even more frequently - but the onus is on us to do more research, more often.

Embracing computerisation, we were gleefully told, would revolutionise production techniques. Up to a point that's true. Twenty years ago we could not have afforded - either temporally or fiscally - to provide you with coloured maps and photography. Nor could we have imagined publishing updated editions of the guides (at least where the most popular routes are concerned) on something approaching an annual basis. Yet that is exactly what we are doing now, and the guide you hold in your hands is an update of the fourth edition first published barely fifteen months ago.

Twenty years ago most canalside villages had a general store, a pub, a telephone kiosk and a bus stop. The shop would have belonged to the same family for generations; the landlord would keep the same hours, sell the same beer and not serve food on a Monday night; the red telephone box would have overlooked the green since it was installed; and the bus would usefully run on market days to the nearest town.

That was then, this is now. The shop's gone; the pub belongs to a non-brewing brewery owned by a Belgian holding company; the all-glass telephone kiosk's been moved three times; and the bus is council-sponsored and operates to a bewildering timetable of little use to man or beast.

Round and round, faster and faster. Small wonder we cling to our canals. We need all the escape routes we can muster.

*Michael Pearson*

Fenny 'Tunnel" on the Oxford Canal.

# The Oxford Canal

Reflections in a lift bridge at Thrupp

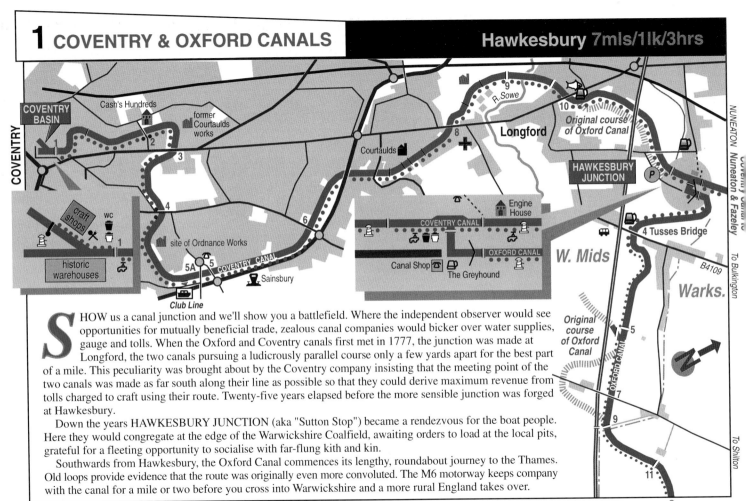

**COVENTRY BASIN**

COVENTRY

Cash's Hundreds

former Courtaulds works

craft shops

WC

historic warehouses

site of Ordnance Works

Club Line

Sainsbury

COVENTRY CANAL

5A    5

R. Sowe

Courtaulds

Longford

Original course of Oxford Canal

HAWKESBURY JUNCTION

P

COVENTRY CANAL

Engine House

OXFORD CANAL

Canal Shop

The Greyhound

W. Mids

Warks.

4 Tusses Bridge

B4109    To Bulkington

Original course of Oxford Canal

OXFORD CANAL

To Shilton

NUNEATON Nuneaton & Fazeley

M6 Southbound

2

**S**HOW us a canal junction and we'll show you a battlefield. Where the independent observer would see opportunities for mutually beneficial trade, zealous canal companies would bicker over water supplies, gauge and tolls. When the Oxford and Coventry canals first met in 1777, the junction was made at Longford, the two canals pursuing a ludicrously parallel course only a few yards apart for the best part of a mile. This peculiarity was brought about by the Coventry company insisting that the meeting point of the two canals was made as far south along their line as possible so that they could derive maximum revenue from tolls charged to craft using their route. Twenty-five years elapsed before the more sensible junction was forged at Hawkesbury.

Down the years HAWKESBURY JUNCTION (aka "Sutton Stop") became a rendezvous for the boat people. Here they would congregate at the edge of the Warwickshire Coalfield, awaiting orders to load at the local pits, grateful for a fleeting opportunity to socialise with far-flung kith and kin.

Southwards from Hawkesbury, the Oxford Canal commences its lengthy, roundabout journey to the Thames. Old loops provide evidence that the route was originally even more convoluted. The M6 motorway keeps company with the canal for a mile or two before you cross into Warwickshire and a more rural England takes over.

A more detailed coverage of the Coventry Arm appears in the SOUTH MIDLANDS Canal Companion

THE Oxford Canal slices through the grain of the countryside like someone cutting an appetising slice of fruit pie. But instead of oozing blackberry and apple filling, a rural landscape of shallow valleys and modest rises is exposed. Canal and railway share an embankment near Brinklow, scene of many well known photographs and paintings depicting narrowboats and steam trains in quaint juxtaposition; tortoise and hare of 19th century transport. This, however, was not the original course of the canal. Reference to the map will indicate just how tortuous that once was. The embankments and cuttings that characterise the northern section of

the Oxford now date from 'shortenings', undertaken between 1829 and 1834, which eliminated no less than fifteen miles between Hawkesbury and Braunston. As surveyed, Brindley's original route stretched the fifteen crow miles between Coventry and Napton into a staggering forty-three miles of convoluted canal. Brindley didn't care. He felt that the more places his canal visited, the more influence and commerce one might accrue. No-one expected canal transport to be fast. Its benefits lay in convenience and reliability. Even after the improvements old sections remained in use serving businesses and wharves already established on their banks.

STRETTON STOP was formerly a point at which tolls were taken. The scene here today is invariably busy and colourful. The old arm to Stretton Wharf is used for private moorings. Boaters should take care not to collide with the foot swing-bridge which links the towpath side with the boatbuilding sheds on the opposite bank. Fosse Way crosses the canal at Bridge 30.

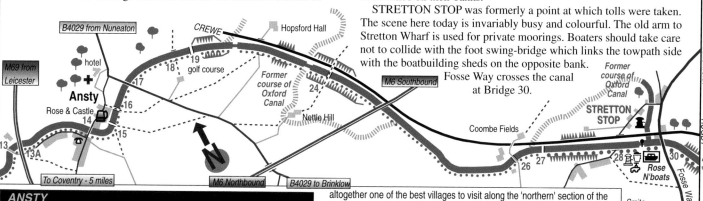

## ANSTY
Shop-less village on outskirts of Coventry, but pleasant moorings and convivial pub in the ROSE & CASTLE (Tel: 024 7661 2822).

## BRINKLOW
Brinklow's agreeably wide main street is framed by a enjoyable miscellany of building styles and periods. At the edge of the village a pair of iron gates denote the location of a former wharf which lay on the old route of the canal. Past the Perpendicular church a lane leads up to the motte & bailey outline of a former Norman castle. Brinklow is altogether one of the best villages to visit along the 'northern' section of the Oxford Canal, but do beware of the Fosse Way traffic.

There are several pubs in Brinklow, notably THE RAVEN (Marston's - Tel: 01788 832655) and the WHITE LION (Bass - Tel: 01788 832579). The village also boasts a fish & chip shop and Chinese takeaway.

The boatyard shop stocks provisions, but also in the village, about ten minutes walk from the canal, you'll find a newsagent, post office and general store, as well as a thriving pottery and several antique shops.

BUSES - regular services to/from Rugby via Newbold; useful staging points for towpath walkers. Tel: 01788 535555.

ROBABLY at its prettiest, the 'Northern Oxford' moves lanquidly from bridge-hole to bridge-hole in no apparent rush to get to Rugby, or anywhere else for that matter. And herein lies perhaps the greatest secret of canal travel: by removing the 'aims' and 'targets' with which we are apt to litter our highly stressed lives, a calmer, stress-free existence emerges, enabling all us inland waterway Houdinis to escape our self-imposed chains and bounds more effectively than those slaves to sun tans on Spanish beaches.

Bridge 32 carries the 'modernised', mid-nineteenth century towpath over the original route, retained as an arm to serve Brinklow. The depth of the 'new' cutting is considerable. It was the work of fledgling engineers Cubitt and Vignoles, both of whom were to make their reputations during the railway era.

At intervals, other sections of the original route join and leave the canal beneath the spans of elegant cast-iron bridges made by the Horseley Iron Works Company of Tipton whose structures proliferate on the BCN. These reedy old arms are, alas, no longer remotely navigable; a shame, they would have made delightful mooring backwaters of considerably more charm than the massive lagoons which have appeared all over the system. Their towpaths have vanished as well, rendering them unexplorable even on foot, though here and there an ancient bridge remains stranded surreaily in the midst of some field or other.

At Newbold those with an enthusiasm for such things can discover one of the portals of the original tunnel at the foot of St Botolph's churchyard. This change of route explains why the "Boat Inn" seems to have nothing to do with the canal whereas it once fronted on to it. The Newbold Arm was kept profitably in water longer than most because it supplied the water troughs on the adjoining railway used by express steam trains to fill their tenders without stopping.

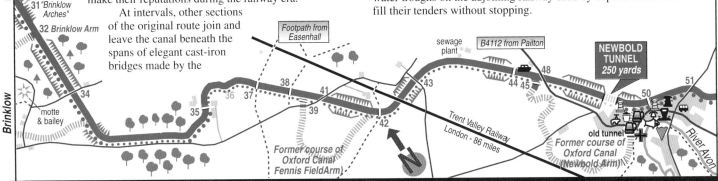

## NEWBOLD-ON-AVON

With its church, canal wharf, and access to the infant River Avon, Newbold is a pleasant enough suburb of Rugby - useful for the replenishment of stores and perhaps some morale-boosting refreshment at one or other of the two pubs.

Adjacent to Newbold Tunnel, THE BOAT (Tel: 01788 576995) and BARLEY MOW (Tel: 01788 544174) compete for canal trade. There is both a fish & chip shop and Balti takeaway in Newbold. alternatively, build up an appetite by walking across the fields from Bridge 37 to Easenhall. It'll take perhaps twenty minutes but the GOLDEN LION (Tel: 01788 832265) makes it well worthwhile.

Large ALLDAYS store incorporating newagency, post office and butcher's shop.

BUSES - frequent weekday service to/from Rugby town centre and Hillmorton, the latter destination being useful for one-way towpath walks. Tel: 01788 535555.

 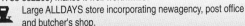

*T*HE saving in distance achieved by the 19th century improvements to the Oxford Canal is nowhere more apparent than in the vicinity of Rugby. In order to keep to the 300ft contour and minimise earthworks, the original route went wandering off a couple of miles to the north, looking for a convenient point to cross the River Swift. Then, having returned to the outskirts of Rugby via Brownsover, it set off again, this time to cross the River Avon near Clifton-on-Dunsmore. Paid by the mile, the contractors must have laughed all the way to the bank.

The outskirts of Rugby are not especially pretty, but neither are they dull. Retail parks, ring roads, industrial units, housing estates and all the other accumulated junk of modern day life are paraded for the canal traveller's contempt. Cubitt's new route involved a sequence of aqueducts and embankments across the wide valleys of the Swift and Avon which form a confluence just to the south. It makes for a fascinating journey to this day, conifers masking the proximity of factories and shops, and there is barely a dull moment as the entrances and exits of the old loops are passed, and you try to do a Sherlock Holmes on the topography of the original canal. A footpath leads enticingly along the old Brownsover Arm. There are lost railways to decipher as well. The Midland, London & North Western and Great Central all converged on Rugby, all crossed the canal, and all fell foul of Beeching. The Stamford and Peterborough line left Rugby on a high, curving viaduct which still looms poignantly over the local golf course.

By road, Rugby and Hillmorton are inseparable. The canal, though, takes its time in travelling between the two, dallying in the fields before a widening, fringed by reed beds, heralds the first of three duplicated locks carrying the canal up past the Oxford Canal Company's dignified workshops, framed by Bridge 70. A craft complex is being developed here whilst, already in business, is the Canal Bridge Stores gift shop by Bridge 71.

Hillmorton's canalscape has a backdrop of wireless masts - a dozen of the tallest being 820ft high - of necessity lit red at night to ward off low-flying aircraft. Rugby Radio Station dates from 1926 and was used to operate the first trans-Atlantic radio telephone link between London and New York. Nowadays the station transmits telecommunications all over the world and also broadcasts time signals on behalf of the Royal Observatory with an accuracy of one second in three thousand years.

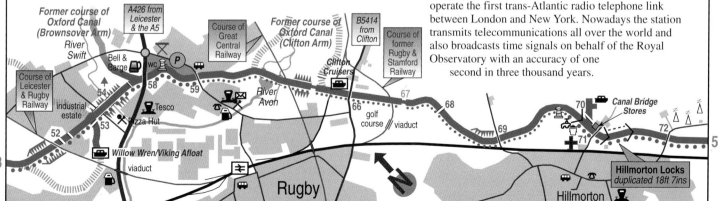

Former course of Oxford Canal (Brownsover Arm)
River Swift
A426 from Leicester & the A5
Course of Great Central Railway
Former course of Oxford Canal (Clifton Arm)
B5414 from Clifton
Course of former Rugby & Stamford Railway
Clifton Cruisers
Bell & Barge
WC
P
Course of Leicester & Rugby Railway
industrial estate
Tesco
Pizza Hut
River Avon
golf course
viaduct
Canal Bridge Stores
Willow Wren/Viking Afloat
viaduct
Rugby
Hillmorton
Hillmorton Locks
duplicated 18ft 7ins
54  58  59  66  67  68  69  70  71  72
52  53
3  5

*Town Centre 1 mile*

## RUGBY

The disappointing fact that the centre of Rugby is such a trek from the canal is no excuse for not taking the trouble to visit this interesting and bustling Warwickshire market town. Rugby's reputation is inextricably linked with its famous public school. Founded in 1567, it wasn't until its best known headmaster, Dr Arnold, arrived on the scene in 1828 that the glory years ensued. Ever since, Rugby has held its place among the top schools in the country, and a steady stream of former pupils have gone on to make their mark on the world. Ironically, it was a boy with possibly less than average intellect who made the greatest gesture of all when, one day in 1823, to alleviate the boredom of a football match, he picked up the ball and ran with it, thereby founding the game of 'rugby'. A plaque in the close adjacent to the school commemorates William Webb Ellis's defiant gesture, whilst nearby stands a statue to Thomas Hughes, former pupil and author of *Tom Brown's Schooldays*. Rugby School's past roll-call is particularly rich in such literary figures, and includes Matthew Arnold (son of the headmaster), 'Lewis Carroll', Walter Savage Landor and Rupert Brooke.

BELL & BARGE - canalside Bridge 58. Harvester Inn plus Holiday Express hotel. Tel: 01788 569466.

PIZZA HUT - located in retail park adjacent aqueduct 54.

SUMMERSAULT - High Street, town centre. Award winning restaurant and coffee house housed in shop also dealing in crafts and clothing. Tel: 01788 543223.

LA CASA LOCO - Little Church Street. Mexican, Texan and Cajun cuisine. Tel: 01788 565756.

All facilities are to be found in the town centre just over a mile south of Bridge 59 (from where there are frequent local buses). Rugby is a comprehensive shopping centre without being overpowering, and in addition to the standard chain stores there are a fair number of long established local retailers. Outdoor markets are held on Mondays, Fridays and Saturdays.

TOURIST INFORMATION - Rugby Visitor Centre, Lawrence Sheriff Street. Tel: 01788 535348.

RUGBY ART GALLERY & MUSEUM - Little Elborow Street. Rugby's latest cultural attraction, featuring modern British art, the Tripontium Collection of Roman artifacts and social history objects relating to the town. Tel: 01788 533721.

RUGBY SCHOOL MUSEUM - Little Church Street. Tel: 01788 556109. Museum open Mon-Sat with guided tours at 2.30pm.

JAMES GILBERT MUSEUM - St Matthews Street. Place of pilgrimage for lovers of the oval balls. Open Mon-Sat. Tel: 01788 333888.

BUSES - services throughout the area - Tel: 01788 535555.
TRAINS - station half a mile south of Bridge 59. Tel: 08457 484950.

**Newbold Tunnel & duckweed - Oxford Canal**

# 5 OXFORD CANAL

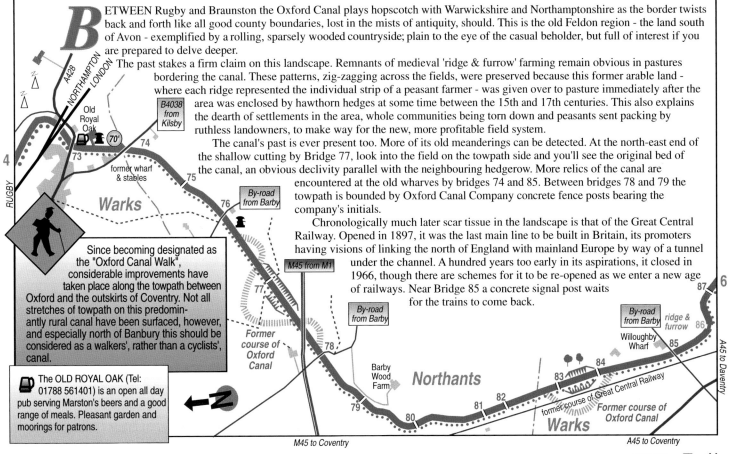

BETWEEN Rugby and Braunston the Oxford Canal plays hopscotch with Warwickshire and Northamptonshire as the border twists back and forth like all good county boundaries, lost in the mists of antiquity, should. This is the old Feldon region - the land south of Avon - exemplified by a rolling, sparsely wooded countryside; plain to the eye of the casual beholder, but full of interest if you are prepared to delve deeper.

The past stakes a firm claim on this landscape. Remnants of medieval 'ridge & furrow' farming remain obvious in pastures bordering the canal. These patterns, zig-zagging across the fields, were preserved because this former arable land - where each ridge represented the individual strip of a peasant farmer - was given over to pasture immediately after the area was enclosed by hawthorn hedges at some time between the 15th and 17th centuries. This also explains the dearth of settlements in the area, whole communities being torn down and peasants sent packing by ruthless landowners, to make way for the new, more profitable field system.

The canal's past is ever present too. More of its old meanderings can be detected. At the north-east end of the shallow cutting by Bridge 77, look into the field on the towpath side and you'll see the original bed of the canal, an obvious declivity parallel with the neighbouring hedgerow. More relics of the canal are encountered at the old wharves by bridges 74 and 85. Between bridges 78 and 79 the towpath is bounded by Oxford Canal Company concrete fence posts bearing the company's initials.

Chronologically much later scar tissue in the landscape is that of the Great Central Railway. Opened in 1897, it was the last main line to be built in Britain, its promoters having visions of linking the north of England with mainland Europe by way of a tunnel under the channel. A hundred years too early in its aspirations, it closed in 1966, though there are schemes for it to be re-opened as we enter a new age of railways. Near Bridge 85 a concrete signal post waits for the trains to come back.

Since becoming designated as the "Oxford Canal Walk", considerable improvements have taken place along the towpath between Oxford and the outskirts of Coventry. Not all stretches of towpath on this predominantly rural canal have been surfaced, however, and especially north of Banbury this should be considered as a walkers', rather than a cyclists', canal.

The OLD ROYAL OAK (Tel: 01788 561401) is an open all day pub serving Marston's beers and a good range of meals. Pleasant garden and moorings for patrons.

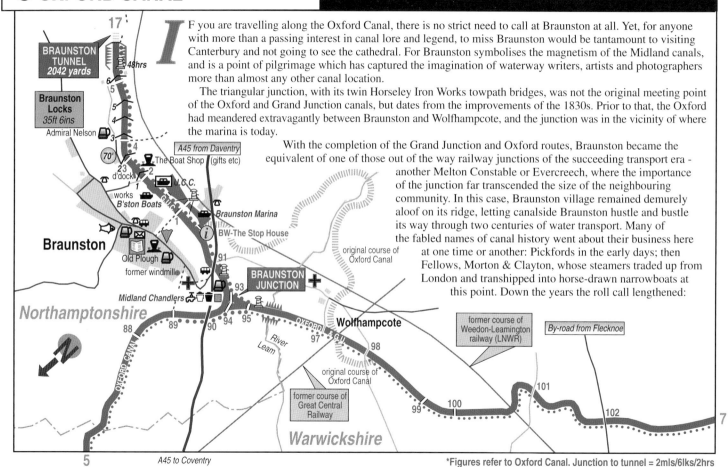

**I**F you are travelling along the Oxford Canal, there is no strict need to call at Braunston at all. Yet, for anyone with more than a passing interest in canal lore and legend, to miss Braunston would be tantamount to visiting Canterbury and not going to see the cathedral. For Braunston symbolises the magnetism of the Midland canals, and is a point of pilgrimage which has captured the imagination of waterway writers, artists and photographers more than almost any other canal location.

The triangular junction, with its twin Horseley Iron Works towpath bridges, was not the original meeting point of the Oxford and Grand Junction canals, but dates from the improvements of the 1830s. Prior to that, the Oxford had meandered extravagantly between Braunston and Wolfhampcote, and the junction was in the vicinity of where the marina is today.

With the completion of the Grand Junction and Oxford routes, Braunston became the equivalent of one of those out of the way railway junctions of the succeeding transport era - another Melton Constable or Evercreech, where the importance of the junction far transcended the size of the neighbouring community. In this case, Braunston village remained demurely aloof on its ridge, letting canalside Braunston hustle and bustle its way through two centuries of water transport. Many of the fabled names of canal history went about their business here at one time or another: Pickfords in the early days; then Fellows, Morton & Clayton, whose steamers traded up from London and transhipped into horse-drawn narrowboats at this point. Down the years the roll call lengthened:

Map labels:

BRAUNSTON TUNNEL 2042 yards
Braunston Locks 35ft 6ins
Admiral Nelson
48hrs
A45 from Daventry
The Boat Shop (gifts etc)
d'dock
U.C.C.
works
B'ston Boats
Braunston
Braunston Marina
BW-The Stop House
Old Plough
former windmill
BRAUNSTON JUNCTION
Midland Chandlers
Northamptonshire
Wolfhampcote
original course of Oxford Canal
original course of Oxford Canal
former course of Weedon-Leamington railway (LNWR)
By-road from Flecknoe
former course of Great Central Railway
River Leam
Warwickshire
A45 to Coventry

*Figures refer to Oxford Canal. Junction to tunnel = 2mls/6lks/2hrs

Nursers, boatbuilders, and painters of arguably the most sublime 'Roses & Castles' ever seen on the system; Samuel Barlow, the coal carriers whose boats were always in the most pristine of condition; and, towards the end, Willow Wren and Blue Line, who kept canal carrying defiantly afloat into the era of the juggernaut.

But the working boats have gone, and with them, inevitably, something of Braunston's old magic. Nevertheless, this is still a flourishing canal centre, home to a hire fleet and a massive marina based on former reservoirs. Wander along the towpath and you'll see new boats being built, old ones restored, and a regular stream of traffic up and down the locks, and it only takes the aroma of a charcoal stove, the beat of a Bolinder, or the rattle of the ratchets in the twilight of an autumn afternoon for the old days to be evoked, making you glad you came.

The former 'Stop House' today serves as British Waterways' area office. It features an information and exhibition area where literature, gifts and advice are dispensed by BW staff proficient in the art of public relations. Meanwhile, six wide beam locks carry the Grand Union up to the mouth of Braunston Tunnel. Water and energy can be saved by working through them in company. Passage in under an hour is

eminently possible given sufficient enthusiasm. Braunston Tunnel takes about twenty minutes to negotiate. What happens at the other end is detailed on Map 17.

The five mile section between Braunston and Napton is interesting scenically and historically. It is a thoroughly remote length of canal; the countryside falling flatly away to the north-west, but climbing abruptly to a notable ridge in the opposite direction. There are ghosts and echoes everywhere: reedy old loops; abandoned railways; lost villages; and, at Wolfhampcote, a 'friendless church'.

When the Grand Union Canal was formed in 1929, there remained a gap between its former Grand Junction (London-Braunston) and Warwick & Napton constituents which belonged to the Oxford Canal. Knowing a good thing when they saw it, the Oxford company kindly allowed the Grand Union to pick up the tab for a programme of dredging and concrete banking, at the same time continuing to extract tolls from them until Nationalisation. A phenomenon relating to this 'joint' length is that boats travelling between the Midlands and the South, via either the Oxford or the Grand Union, pass each other going in the opposite direction; shades of the Great Western and Southern railways at Exeter.

## BRAUNSTON

Village Braunston straddles its ridge, four hundred feet up on the slopes of the Northamptonshire uplands. Enclosed fields, still bearing the pattern of ridge & furrow, distil the spirit of the Middle Ages. Sauntering along the High Street from the village green to the tall spired church, one encounters a mixture of stone and brick buildings, including a sail-less and now residential windmill and a 17th century manor house.

At the foot of a long hill the A45 crosses the canal. This was the Chester turnpike road which became part of Telford's route from London to Holyhead. There was a tollhouse here at the foot of a winding and precipitous descent from Daventry. During the Second World War a considerable number of evacuees were billeted in the village which, at that time, had only just received the benefits of electricity. Now, handsome modern flats overlook the marina, and Braunston must be as busy and as populated as never before, though it contrives to evoke a timeless air which has much to commend it.

THE MILL HOUSE - canalside Bridge 91. Family pub and restaurant with customer moorings and children's garden.Tel: 01788 890450.
THE OLD PLOUGH - High Street. One of two village locals, this one serves Ansell's beers and fine meals. Tel: 01788 890000.
ADMIRAL NELSON - canalside Bridge 4. Popular, refurbished canalside inn. Restaurant and bar meals, attractive garden. Tel: 01788 890075.
Fish & chips in the village.

How nice to stroll through a village shopping! Facilities include: GURNEY'S well-stocked general store and newsagency; a butcher, post office and bakery still displaying an old fashioned 'Hovis' sign. Down by the canal, by the bottom lock, THE BOAT SHOP opens from 8am-8pm throughout the summer season and deals in just about everything from gifts to groceries.

BUSES - Geoff Amos Coaches to/from Rugby and Daventry. Tel: 01327 702181. Mon-Sat service, useful for towpath walks from Rugby to Braunston.

**A**T Napton Junction (known to working boatmen as Wigrams Turn) the Oxford Canal sets off southwards on its long, winding road to the Thames. Despite the proximity of two busy marinas, the junction itself is typically remote. A 1930s concrete bridge spans the entrance and exit of the Grand Union route, formerly the Warwick & Napton Canal. Interestingly, it is numbered 17. Where (we can hear you wondering) are the other sixteen? The answer is that they were in the Grand Union Company's imagination. When they acquired rights to the route from Braunston to Birmingham in 1929 they re-numbered the sequence of bridges from Braunston northwards, including those on the Oxford Canal as far as Napton which never actually bore the GU numbers allocated to them.

East of Napton the shared section of the Oxford and Grand Union routes pursues its lonely course, passing the small settlement of Lower Shuckburgh and its picturesque Victorian church. A footpath climbs from here through parkland to the medieval village of Upper Shuckburgh. The name is said to mean 'a hill haunted by goblins'. Certainly Beacon Hill, rising to 678 feet, has its spirits. A 17th century member of the Shuckburgh family is said to have been accosted by King Charles I whilst hunting on the hill. The King, on his way to fight at the Battle of Edgehill, demanded to know how an English gentleman could spare time for hunting when his King was fighting for his crown.

Whilst the Grand Union heads determinedly off towards Birmingham, the more poetically minded Oxford picks its way quietly around the skirts of Napton Hill, a gentle summit half eaten away by old quarry workings. For the best part of a century clay was extracted from the hill and used in the manufacture of bricks at the works by Bridge 112. Narrowboats carried the finished products to Napton railway station on the Warwick & Napton Canal a couple of miles north of Napton Junction. Nowadays the site of the works is occupied by various light industries, including Peter Nicholls' busy boatbuilding yard.

NAPTON LOCKS lift the canal up to the hamlet of Marston Doles. With a

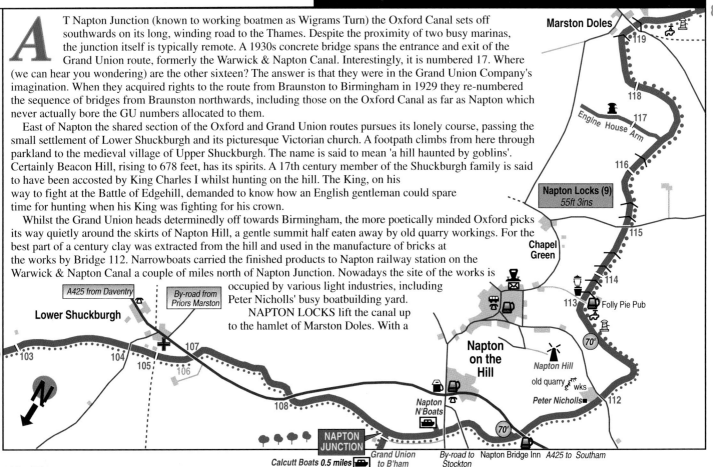

well-surfaced towpath and a lock-wheeling lock-keeper (at busy times at any rate) the flight seems a snip; though at the height of summer there may be queues. The 'Napton and Marston Doles Backpumping Scheme' has improved water supply to the canal's summit level. Napton's famous windmill is a constant landmark, whilst in the lengthy pound between the top two locks and the rest a branch canal leaves the main line and appears to head off across the fields towards Beacon Hill. This is the Engine House Arm, dug to enable boats to bring coal to a stationary steam engine which once pumped water through a system of channels and pipes back to the summit section; the arm is now in use as a backwater for linear moorings. The top lock is overlooked by a handsome, trapezium-shaped warehouse nowadays in use as offices.

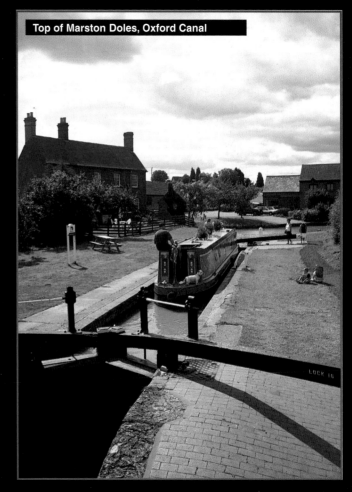

Top of Marston Doles, Oxford Canal

## NAPTON ON THE HILL

Napton (best reached from Bridge 113) basks in the sunshine (and occasionally gales) on its south-facing hill. Its street pattern takes some fathoming, but there is much green space between the houses and even the seemingly obligatory modern developments dovetail neatly into the whole. You can climb towards the windmill for a better view, but it is never open to the public.

THE BRIDGE AT NAPTON - canalside Bridge 111. Bar & restaurant meals and pleasant garden. Tel: 01926 812466.

THE FOLLY PIE PUB - adjacent Bridge 113. Long ago known as "The Bull & Butcher", and relicensed after many dry years in 1990, this is now a boater-friendly pub serving an excellent range of meals. Tel: 01926 815185.

Napton lies half a mile east of Bridge 113 with a post office stores catering for most requirements. The Folly Canal Shop, adjacent to the pub, sells basic provisions and souvenirs. Cycle hire from 'Off the Beaten Track' - Tel: 01926 817380.

BUSES - useful links with Leamington Spa for towpath walkers. Tel: 01788 535555.

## FENNY COMPTON WHARF *(Map 8)*

THE WHARF - canalside Bridge 136. Marston's, Bass and Fuller's ales plus bar and restaurant meals. Tel: 01295 770332.

WHARF STORES - canalside Bridge 136. Groceries, newspapers and gifts throughout the cruising season.

# 8 OXFORD CANAL

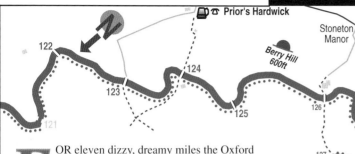

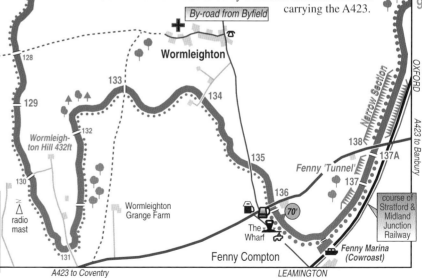

**Prior's Hardwick**

Stoneton Manor

Berry Hill 600ft

122
124
123
125
126
7
121
127

**F**OR eleven dizzy, dreamy miles the Oxford Canal traverses its depopulated summit. With a compass, a pair of stout walking shoes and a healthy disregard for the laws of trespass, you could do it in four. But because - as the poet Edward Thomas put it - "there is nothing at the end of any road better than can be found beside it" - you feel no desire to count the miles, no temptation to begrudge Brindley his watershed wanderings. We used to say that the Oxford's summit was as shallow as a matinee idol's smile, but dredging has increased the depth of water available and it is now perfectly feasible to average something in the region of three miles an hour.

The loneliness of the summit has a mystic, trance-inducing quality. From time to time you may catch glimpses of another boat

Hikers on the OXFORD CANAL WALK are faced with a number of shortcut opportunities(Bridges 133 to 128 for instance). Some of the summit towpath, once infamously incomplete, has still to be properly surfaced (and is thus not comfortably cyclable) but walking is no problem now.

on what appears to be a neighbouring waterway, and you take some convincing before accepting that this is really a boat ahead of you, or behind you, on the same convoluted canal. Shades of the Leeds & Liverpool Canal's Marton Pool.

Wormleighton sleeps the sleep of the innocent on a gentle slope overlooking the canal's meanderings. Chief delight is the gatehouse dating from 1613, built from local stone the colour of a weatherbeaten face. South of the wharf at Fenny Compton (see page 15) the canal negotiates a deep, narrow cutting. When the canal was first built there was a thousand yard tunnel here. But the rock was brittle and the bore a bottleneck, and in time the top was taken off. Bridge 137A is an elegant cast iron turnover bridge carrying the towpath from one side to the other. It is dwarfed by a modern concrete structure carrying the A423.

By-road from Byfield
**Wormleighton**
9
128
133
134
129
132
Wormleigh-ton Hill 432ft
135
138
137A
Fenny 'Tunnel'
130
136
137
OXFORD
A423 to Banbury
Wormleighton Grange Farm
70'
course of Stratford & Midland Junction Railway
radio mast
131
The Wharf
Fenny Marina (Cowroast)
Fenny Compton
A423 to Coventry
LEAMINGTON

SOUTHBOUND, the Oxford begins its long, drawn out descent to the Thames. Northwards, CLAYDON marks the start of the summit section; no more locks to work for four or five hours! Wormleighton, Boddington and Clattercote are not, as you might assume, a firm of Banbury solicitors, but rather the three reservoirs which feed the Oxford Canal. Water shortages have always been a problem on this waterway and at times the density of pleasure traffic exacerbates the situation, forcing British Waterways to restrict the opening hours of locks; a practice of dubious logic, arguaby concentrating usage rather than reducing it, though at least it allows staff to ensure that no careless boaters leave paddles up overnight.

Bridge 141 straddles the county boundary and is the northernmost of the characteristic draw bridges synonymous with this canal. They are

simplicity defined, consisting of no more than a pair of shallow brick abutments, a platform and two hefty timber balance beams set at 45 degrees when the bridge is closed to boats, or flat against the nettles when, as is often the case, they are left open. Seen from afar, they punctuate the Oxford Canal's passage through the Cherwell Valley, as homogeneous with this landscape as the pollarded willows of its watermeadows and the oolite stonework of its villages.

The course of the old Stratford & Midland Junction Railway parallels the canal by Bridge 142 which spans the feeder from Boddington Reservoir. The railway was one of those forgotten little lines whose high hopes were never realised. It became disparagingly, but affectionately known as the 'Slow, Mouldy and Jolting'. L.T.C. Rolt loved the unhurried progress of its trains, their "slow, panting climbs, and swift, swaying descents" across the Northamptonshire uplands. Brian Collings, our cover artist, travelled on the line's last passenger train in 1952.

At CLAYDON TOP LOCK, the Oxford Canal Company built workshops and stables. This would have been a busy spot in the heyday

*Continued on page 18*

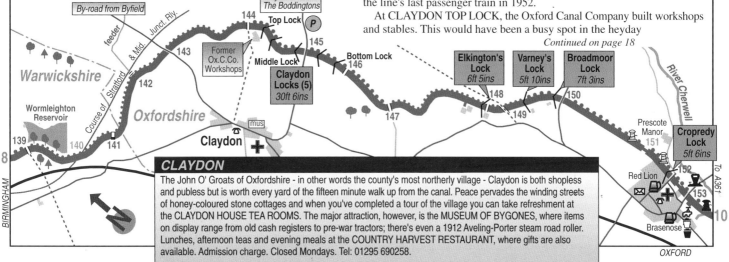

### CLAYDON

The John O' Groats of Oxfordshire - in other words the county's most northerly village - Claydon is both shopless and publess but is worth every yard of the fifteen minute walk up from the canal. Peace pervades the winding streets of honey-coloured stone cottages and when you've completed a tour of the village you can take refreshment at the CLAYDON HOUSE TEA ROOMS. The major attraction, however, is the MUSEUM OF BYGONES, where items on display range from old cash registers to pre-war tractors; there's even a 1912 Aveling-Porter steam road roller. Lunches, afternoon teas and evening meals at the COUNTRY HARVEST RESTAURANT, where gifts are also available. Admission charge. Closed Mondays. Tel: 01295 690258.

*Continued from page 17*

of the canal. The buildings have now been restored for use as a private dwelling and a highly desirable one at that. Three isolated locks interrupt the canal's otherwise uneventful progress between Claydon and Cropredy. Elkington's Lock is overlooked by a subtly extended farmhouse; Varney's Lock bisects ridge & furrow field patterns; and at Broadmoor Lock a fender maker plys his trade. The old wharf at CROPREDY looked slightly down-at-heel when we last passed by, although the warehouse still has gainful employment as the base of the Banbury Canoe Club. The canal itself narrows by the old toll office and manager's house, whilst south of Bridge 153 a former coal wharf provides room to turn a seventy footer. Visitor moorings are provided north of Cropredy Lock, a pleasant base from which to savour the delights of this lovely village.

## CROPREDY (Map 9)

Cropredy is the village with the closest relationship to the Oxford Canal and, as such, makes an ideal place to break your journey, whether on foot or afloat. In recent years it has become famous in folk music circles as the location of an annual (in August) festival centred round the enduring folk rock group *Fairport Convention*. But this is one music festival where locals and visitors seem in harmony: the "Brasenose Inn" even features on the cover of one of Fairport's albums.

You have to go back over three hundred years to the other most significant event in Cropredy's mellow existence. There was a Civil War battle here in 1644. Ten thousand men took part and some of the clobber they left behind - helmets, bayonets and cannon balls - is on display in the church, along with a pre-Reformation brass lectern which was apparently submerged in the Cherwell to keep it safe from the marauding Puritans.

THE RED LION - adjacent Bridge 152. Thatched village inn visited by Temple Thurston (*The Flower of Gloster*) and L.T.C. Rolt (*Narrow Boat*). It has lost none of its charm. Sunbeams still slant through the neighbouring churchyard and glint on your pint of Wadworth 6X. Good range of food usually available. Families welcome. Tel: 01295 758239.

THE BRASENOSE INN - 300 yards west of Bridge 153. Classic country local offering Bass, bar and restaurant meals. Tel: 01295 750244.

OLD COAL WHARF - by Bridge 153. Teas, coffees and light meals in old coal merchant's premises. Tel: 01295 750878.

THE GREEN SCENE - Cropredy Green. Coffees, light lunches and afternoon teas. Tel: 01295 758085.

BRIDGE STORES by Bridge 153 is open daily stocking groceries, wines & spirits, newspapers, gifts and Calor gas. Deeper into the village you'll come across a post office (early closing Wed & Sat) and the 'Green Scene' gallery and coffee shop.

BUSES - infrequent (but useful for one way towpath walks) service connects with Banbury. Tel: 01327 702181.

## BANBURY (Map 10)

Once an Oxfordshire market town, now seemingly an extension of London's commuterland, Banbury is a useful place for shopping, replenishing the wallet and stocking up on tourist literature at the excellent TIC. Since construction of the M40, Banbury has brightened-up its act and takes more pride in its appearance than the world-weary, traffic-blighted place it used to be. The streets are cleaner and more revealing of the pleasant architecture surviving from its heyday as a bustling country town. Our favourite building is the former corn merchants by the market place, its upper storey a signwritten reminder of Banbury's importance as an agricultural centre - it still has a massive cattle market on the outskirts, handy for the motorway. Neither has the town forgotten its niche in the pantheon of nursery rhymes, and a replica cross (erected by the Victorians following removal of the original by a Puritan mob in 1600) can still be seen at the southern end of The Horsefair.

It would have been nice to see some good restaurants materialising canalside within the Castle Quay development. COSTAS coffee bar is inexplicably inside - we would have liked to lounge with our ice lattes at waterside tables. Further into town you'll discover a plethora of pubs, cafes and ethnic restaurants. Try the stylish CHURCH HOUSE BRASIERE (Tel: 01295 265466) or the THAI ORCHID (Tel: 01295 270833), both on North Bar, or YE OLDE REINDEER INN (Tel: 01295 264031), Banbury's oldest inn dating from 1570. EXCHANGE on High Street (Tel: 01295 259035) is a Wetherspoon's post office conversion. BANESBERIE'S (Tel: 01295 269066) is a tea room on Butchers Row.

The spanking new canalside CASTLE QUAY shopping centre likes to think that it's put Milton Keynes in its place. Certainly as far as canal travellers are concerned there's no excuse for not laying in stores. One can't help but notice, however, that the new centre has drained some of the vitality out of the town's old streets where a surprising amount of early closing occurs on Tuesday afternoons. Thursday and Saturday are market days. Authentic Banbury cakes are on sale at a number of outlets, including the TIC.

MUSEUM & TOURIST INFORMATION - The Horsefair. Tel: 01295 259855. Well stocked, helpful staff and local history. (*Moving canalside 2001*)

BUSES - services throughout the area. Tel: 01295 253451.

TRAINS - services to/from Oxford, Leamington, London & Birmingham. Tel: 08457 484950.

AT Cropredy the Oxford Canal makes eye contact with the River Cherwell, but like all good bodice-rippers, the affair takes many twists and turns before consumation takes place. The canal company purchased Cropredy Mill and adapted the mill stream to provide the canal with water. Slat Mill, wherever it stood, whatever it ground, has long gone. With the river and railway as companions, the canal progresses uneventfully through a rural landscape. By Hardwick Lock the M40 motorway makes its northernmost crossing of the canal. Below the lock, and overlooked by a large aluminium plant, the canal parallels the course of the Oxfordshire Ironstone Railway built by German prisoners of the First World War to access the ironstone quarries west of Banbury. Part of its trackbed, along with several miles of towpath, is included in the "Banbury Fringe Circular Walk".

Banbury sits like a bad bruise on the peaches and cream complexion of the Oxford Canal. For two or three turgid miles the picturesque images usually associated with this canal are invaded by ring-roads, factories and urban sprawl. But paradoxically, one can't help but feel grateful for a change of scene: all those meadows and wooded ridges can be a bit unremitting when encountered at three miles an hour. Welcome to the fleshpots!

Trade on the Oxford Canal petered out towards the end of the 1950s. Amongst the last regular cargoes were timber and tar. Up until this time Banbury supported its own canal community who were wont to congregate at a spit and sawdust pub called "The Struggler". L.T.C. Rolt immortalised it in his *Inland Waterways of England*. The pub and the canal wharf were demolished in 1962 by the local council, who added insult to injury by building a bus station on the site. Now the whole area has been redeveloped into the Castle Quay Shopping Centre and Rolt may well be looking down from heaven and chuckling - with irony. By all means commemorate the great man - but on a *road* bridge! At least Tooley's drydock, also made famous by Rolt as the scene of *Cressy's* docking and refitting prior to the cruise of 1939 recounted in *Narrow Boat*, is to be preserved as part of the new Banbury Museum, due to open its doors to the public in 2001.

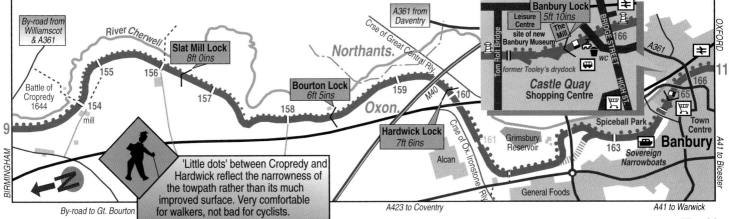

'Little dots' between Cropredy and Hardwick reflect the narrowness of the towpath rather than its much improved surface. Very comfortable for walkers, not bad for cyclists.

**D**RAW bridges abound, their functional looks disguising the economy of construction inherent in their design. Most of them will be chained 'open' and thus of no hindrance to boaters. Another worthwhile cost-cutting measure south of Banbury was the provision of single bottom gates for each lock chamber as opposed to the more usual mitred pairs.

The spire of Kings Sutton church soars above the watermeadows and keeps you company for an hour or two. The village boasts a railway station, but its other facilities are a bit of a hike away on the far side of the Cherwell, which forms the boundary between Oxon and Northants. A plume of smoke issues from the fertilizer works at Twyford Mill. Gas and diesel are available at TWYFORD WHARF.

Kings Sutton Lock is delightful. The keeper's cottage is simply built of brick with stone facing. On the opposite bank stands a former blacksmith's forge and stable block. South of here the canal momentarily sheds its man-made character. The branches of pollarded willows hang caressingly over the water and poplars whisper in the breeze as a belt of woodland is encountered. Into this exquisite

landscape the M40 intrudes like a kick in the groin. When it was being constructed the *Sunday Times* ran a sequence of photographs looking out over the Cherwell Valley in the vicinity of Kings Sutton. It was a sobering illustration of the assassination of the Oxfordshire landscape. As hideous in its way as the sort of photographs they show of bodies in the streets after a military coup. As the Department of Transport used to boast, road schemes such as the M40 had their viability tested on a 'cost benefit basis'. Yes, we know: for the road lobby's benefit at the countryside's cost.

But how long before the motorway is outmoded like the canal itself and the now dismantled Banbury & Cheltenham Railway? The canal can be said to have functioned commercially for over a hundred and fifty years. The railway was relatively shortlived, opening in 1887 and closing to passengers in 1951, though surviving in goods use for another thirteen years. Its most celebrated train was the *Ports to Ports Express*, a service designed to effect the transfer of merchant seamen between Tyneside and South Wales. Did they, catching a glimpse of passing 'joshers', feel momentarily at home on their ten hour, landlocked journey?

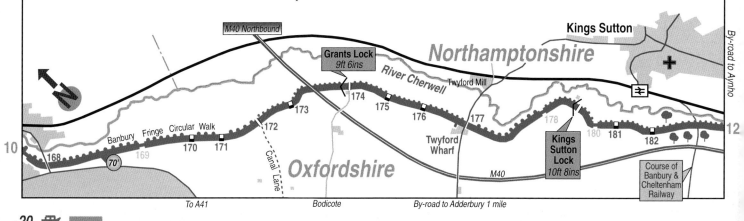

# locks

**Top left:** Aynho Weir Lock
**Top right:** Cropredy Lock
**Lower left:** Somerton Lock
**Lower centre:** Bourton Lock
**Lower right:** King's Sutton Lock

locks

**P**ASSING briefly into Northamptonshire, the canal shares much of this part of its journey with the adjoining railway, but loses little of its tranquillity in the process. Wharves past and present recall the canal's original purpose. The one at AYNHO remains remarkably intact, its brick warehouse being home to a shop selling canal souvenirs, confectionary and a modest range of provisions. For a wider choice walk a country mile uphill to Aynho itself, an enchanting village of narrow winding lanes and a jumble of stone cottages which come in every conceivable shape and size. Go in the spring, when the cherry blossom is in full bloom, to see it at its best.

Aynho's long closed railway station is of Brunellian design, dating from the inception of the original mixed gauge line between Oxford and Birmingham. When the Great Western Railway shaved twenty miles off their London to Birmingham route in 1910, Aynho marked the northern end of the 'cut off'. The lofty viaducts of the new line (now revitalised by Chiltern Trains) form a handsome backdrop to the canal.

Having played coquettishly with the canal's affections since Cropredy, the Cherwell acquires carnal knowledge by Aynho Weir Lock as the channel flows directly across the canal - shameless hussy. The lock itself is shallow and diamond-shaped, Somerton being so deep that extra capacity had to be built into Aynho.

SOMERTON DEEP LOCK is, well, *very* deep. Overlooked by an exceptionally pretty cottage, it vies with Tardebigge on the Worcester & Birmingham for the honour of being the deepest narrowbeam chamber on the canal system. Certainly the steerer's eye view of things, when the lock is empty, is reminiscent of an elephant trap. Heaven knows how single-handed boat captains managed in the past. Tom Foxon hinted at his methods in *Number One*, also relating how it was his habit to swap lumps of coal with the lock-keeper in exchange for fresh laid eggs and a rabbit or two. Those were the days!

Down Somerton way the towpath becomes more of a footpath, a pleasant change for walkers, but somewhat bumpy for cyclists.

## AYNHO

GREAT WESTERN ARMS - Aynho Wharf. Railway memorabilia plus Hook Norton ale and bar meals. Tel: 01869 338288.

AYNHO WHARF - boatyard (see also page 76) with shop selling gifts and groceries. Also snack bar dispensing tea, coffee etc.

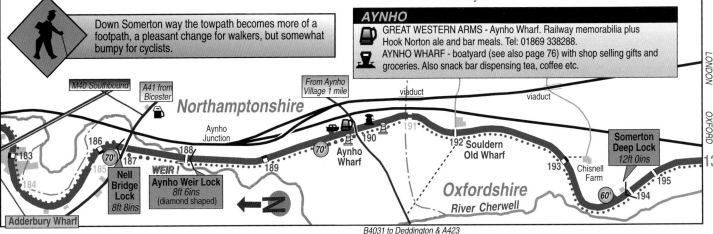

CANAL, railway and river saunter along the valley floor, but the roads keep cautiously to the shoulders of the hills. When the Cherwell bursts its banks in winter, the escaping water forms an inland sea and wildfowl find this an attractive wintering ground. In spring the meadows seem full of lapwings carrying out their dizzy courtship.

Between Somerton and Heyford the canal assumes the character of a river. The towpath loses its formality, becoming more of a track through the adjoining fields. Pollarded willows line the canal's banks, just as they do the Cherwell's, so that seen from a passing train, it is often difficult to tell immediately which is which.

Joni Mitchell's dream has come true - 'the bombers in the sky have turned to butterflies' - now that the giant American airbase at Upper Heyford has been mothballed. The absence of aircraft renders the Cherwell Valley uncannily quiet. Strange how the end of the Cold War should spread ripples to this peaceful corner of Oxfordshire.

Between the two Heyfords the canal arcs deliciously through a belt of woodland. There are glimpses of an attractive cluster of stone buildings - a church, manor house and 15th century tithe barn - below Allen's Lock. Lower Heyford Mill ceased working at the end of the Second World War. Lift-bridge No. 205 is said to have been built of iron to take the weight of the miller's traction engine.

HEYFORD WHARF is very similar to Aynho (Map 12), but on this occasion the warehouse is built of local stone. Nowadays it is in use as a hire base. Heyford railway station stands usefully alongside Bridge 206. A short walk from here lies Rousham House and its famous gardens, which are open to the public all year round. The 17th century house is open to the public on Wednesday and Sunday afternoons between April and September. Children and dogs are not encouraged! For details telephone 01869 347110. Another worthwhile walk is to the charming village of Steeple Aston where the "Red Lion" comes highly recommended.

## THE HEYFORDS

THE BELL - Market Square, Lower Heyford. Charming and peaceful inn overlooking the village's former market place. A good range of ales, plus meals served lunchtimes and evenings. Tel: 01869 347176.
BARLEY MOW - Somerton Road, Upper Heyford. Access from Allen's Lock. Pleasant village local serving Fullers and bar meals. Tel: 01869 232300.

Both Upper and Lower Heyford have lost their shops in recent years, the flipside, one imagines, of the 'peace dividend'.
TRAINS - Thames Trains local services along the Cherwell Valley. Useful staging-post for towpath walks. Details on 08457 484950.

THE Oxford Canal is arguably at its most charming and sublime between Heyford and Thrupp. It drifts through the delicious landscape of the Cherwell Valley like something out of the slow heart of a concerto.

At Northbrook the canal bridge abuts a much older structure spanning the river. This carried a packhorse route across the Cherwell centuries before the canal was even thought of. A mile or two to the south lies the course of the Romans' Akeman Street which linked Cirencester and St Albans.

Immediately south of the course of the Roman road, the canal passes through a dark, emerald tunnel of overhanging trees, which retains an almost primeval quality that the legions must have been familiar, if not exactly at ease, with. In the heart of the wood lie the enigmatic ruins of an old cement works. The canal formed the only practical access to and from the site. Coal, sand and gypsum were brought in by boat and cement taken out, much of it travelling only as far as Enslow where it was transhipped to rail. The works closed in 1927, production being transferred to a new plant - itself now largely demolished - adjacent to Baker's Lock.

There used to be a pub called "The Three Pigeon's" by Bridge 213; hence the name of the adjoining lock. It must have been a welcome resort for the thirsty cement workers, but a long time has passed since the last pint was supped, though the building remains as a private residence, as does another of the Cherwell's former watermills. It's an idyllic quarter of an hour's walk from here - over sluice gates, millstreams and backwaters, and through cornfields - to the sleepy village of Tackley; well worth the walk for its pair of pubs, general stores, post office and railway station replete with replica gas lamps.

Just beneath the railway bridge at Enslow you can see old mooring rings set in the wall and the scars of unloading apparatus where the cement was transhipped from boats into railway wagons. By Bridge 216 stands the popular "Rock of Gibraltar" pub.

Below Baker's Lock the canal merges with the river and sharp bends abound on the reach down to Shipton Weir Lock (Map 15).

When the Cherwell is in flood this can be a hair-raising interlude for the boater.

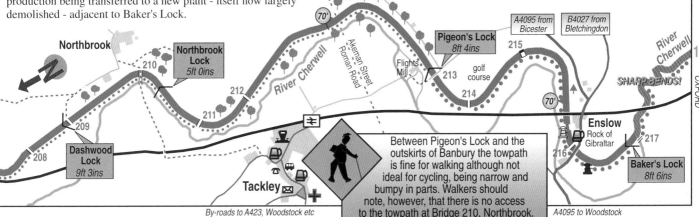

former quarry

Northbrook

70'

River Cherwell

Akeman Street / Roman Road

Northbrook Lock 5ft 0ins

210

212

211

209

208

Dashwood Lock 9ft 3ins

13

Tackley

By-roads to A423, Woodstock etc

Flights Mill

213

golf course

214

Pigeon's Lock 8ft 4ins

215

A4095 from Bicester

B4027 from Bletchingdon

River Cherwell 15

SHARP BENDS!

OXFORD

70'

Enslow Rock of Gibraltar

216

217

Baker's Lock 8ft 6ins

A4095 to Woodstock

Between Pigeon's Lock and the outskirts of Banbury the towpath is fine for walking although not ideal for cycling, being narrow and bumpy in parts. Walkers should note, however, that there is no access to the towpath at Bridge 210, Northbrook.

AT Shipton Weir Lock canal and river part company, the Cherwell flowing south-eastwards past Islip to become that traditionally romantic stream of The Parks with its punts and its poets. Shipton Lock, like Aynho, is diamond shaped and not at all deep, but it can look as welcoming as a Cornish harbour in a gale when the navigable reach of the Cherwell is in spate. It is a remote spot, the old lock-keeper's cottage having been long ago demolished. Boaters from the local club at Thrupp use the backwater for picnics.

Lovers of ecclesiastical architecture will relish viewing the churches at Shipton and Hampton Gay. In the latter's graveyard a headstone commemorates one of the thirty-four passengers who died in the Christmas Eve railway tragedy of 1874 , when a derailed train plunged into the icy waters of the neighbouring canal. Between bridges 220 and 221 the canal widens into a shadowy lagoon fringed by beds of water lilies and reeds. The canal builders are said to have diverted a millstream here and used its course to form the canal. Onomatopoetically not unlike the sound of a boat engine, Thrupp consists of little more than a waterway maintenance yard housed in handsome buildings of thatch and honey-coloured stone, and a terrace of cottages fronting the canal as though it was a village street. This idyllic setting features as the location for a grisly murder in the Inspector Morse mystery *The Riddle of the Third Mile*. Colin Dexter also used the Oxford Canal in another Morse story, *The Wench is Dead*.

Thrupp might have become an important canal junction had 18th century proposals for a direct link between Hampton Gay and London ever got off the drawing board. The scheme was promoted in rivalry to the Grand Junction Canal and came about largely because of the poor state of the Thames at the time. In the event the Grand Junction received its Royal Assent first and the London & Western Canal, as it was to be known, languished, its subscribers receiving only sixpence back in the pound on their misplaced investment and optimism.

### THRUPP

THE BOAT - Thrupp. A pub which features in many a canaller's 'Desert Island" choice of waterside inns. Sadly Morrells beer is no longer brewed in Oxford but in Dorset now! Nice garden, children welcome. Tel: 01865 374279.
JOLLY BOATMAN - canalside Bridge 223. Main road pub, also popular with boaters. Bar and restaurant meals, Morrell's ales. Canalside seating area, families welcome. Tel: 01865 373775.

### KIDLINGTON

Heavily suburbanised village on the northern periphery of Oxford. Useful for a quick ram-raid on its facilities, but not somewhere you'd choose to moor for any length of time.
WISE ALDERMAN - canalside Bridge 224. Family pub with pleasant garden. Tel: 01865 372281.
Co-op supermarket, shops and banks less than ten minutes walk from bridges 226 and 228. Spar shop close to Bridge 224.

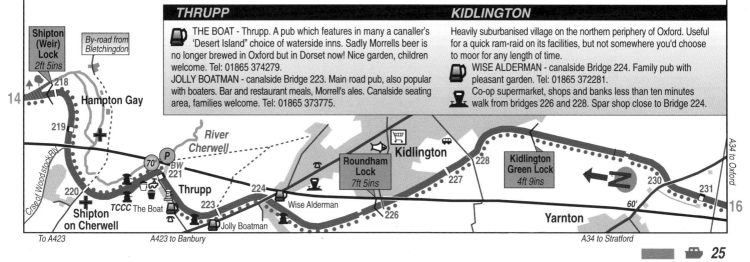

Pretty moorings, at Thrupp on the Oxford Canal

THE canal's approach to (and exit from) the university city of Oxford is low key. Not for it the ethereal landscapes of the Thames and Port Meadow or the Cherwell and The Parks. But rather - with the diffidence of a freshman arriving for Michaelmas Term - it slinks into Oxford by the tradesmens' entrance, making its way modestly past the foot of gardens belonging to the Victorian villas of North Oxford's erudite suburbs.

Coming south from Dukes Lock the countryside seems reluctant to take its cue and leave. Allotments and small holdings border the canal, as do a considerable number of residential boats. Gradually the suburbs begin to make their presence felt: the playing fields of St Edward's School; the imposing redbrick houses

of well-healed dons; a factory discreetly making parts for motor cars. Bridge 240 offers egress to Aristotle Lane, a useful general store, childrens' playground and "The Anchor", and there may be some boaters who prefer to moor here away from the canal's crowded end.

Lucy's foundry is as old as the canal. Once they would cast you anything in iron you cared to mention; nowadays their order books are filled with car components. St Barnabus's church tower was being stone-washed when we did our research trip. Moor here, where British Waterways provide 48 hours free moorings, and its lugubrious chime will invade your beauty-sleep. On the opposite bank, the terraced streets of Jericho (scene of another Morse murder enquiry) are fronted by the boatyard of College Cruisers.

An elegant cast iron bridge spans the entrance to LOUSE LOCK as the main line of the canal heads for its quiet oblivion, a couple

continued on page 28

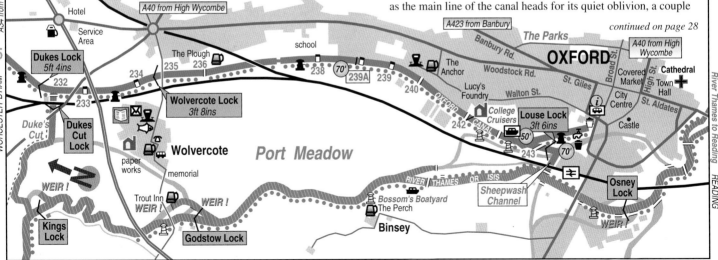

15

of hundred yards or so further on. Once upon a time the Oxford Canal terminated more grandiloquently in a broad basin of busy wharves overlooked by the castle keep. Business was brisk in coal brought down the cut from Warwickshire, and Temple Thurston came here in search of Eynsham Harry. But in 1937 the site was acquired by William Morris, alias Lord Nuffield, for the erection of a new college in his name. Since then the Oxford Canal has not so much terminated as petered out (although there is a scheme to recreate the terminus) and, as the last few yards are (inexplicably) occupied by residential boats, the visiting boater has no alternative but to moor somewhere back between bridges 239 and 243.

Turning needs to be considered as well. Only the shortest of vessels (say 35ft) may turn where the water, rubbish and Elsan disposal facilities are perversely sited at the end of the canal; 50ft and under can turn in the winding hole by Bridge 243; anything longer than that and you'll have to go down through Louse Lock into one of the Thames backwaters to turn. Having got that far, it's difficult to resist the temptation to find your way out of Oxford via the Thames and Duke's Cut. To do this you'll need a Thames short stay licence, which may be acquired from the keeper at Osney Lock, just a short walk south of the railway station. Suitably armed, you can proceed along the Sheepwash Channel (where sadly the yeoman of Oxfordshire no longer gather to dip their flocks) and pass beneath the railway; noticing, as you do, the rusty remains of a railway swingbridge which used to carry the line to the old London & North Western terminus on Rewley Road. Beyond the railway the channel emerges to join the Thames itself. You should turn right, upstream in the direction of Binsey and Godstow and Kings locks.

The next reach is spellbinding. Soon the tree-lined banks open out to expose the full extent of Port Meadow where cattle and horses graze against a skyline of Oxford's dreaming spires. GODSTOW LOCK intervenes, but then it's worth mooring to the grassy bank upstream of Godstow's ancient stone bridge to explore the ruins of the nunnery where Henry II's mistress, Fair Rosamund, died. Or, considering the needs of the inner man, repairing to the famous "Trout Inn" overlooking the adjacent weir stream.

The Thames, also known as Isis hereabouts, meanders from Godstow to KING'S LOCK, and though you may have already fallen for its riverine ways, to regain the canal you must turn right above the lock and head back to the man made waterway. The Duke's Cut was actually the original link between the canal and the river, being opened in 1789. It was owned by the Duke of Marlborough, hence the name. Boats also used it to gain access to Wolvercote paper mill, which relied on boat-loads of Warwickshire coal until 1951. All too soon, passing beneath the A40 and the railway, the little DUKE'S CUT LOCK returns you to the Oxford Canal and reality.

**The Thames (or Isis!) at Port Meadow**

Oxford reminds you of an exclusive club. The best the casual visitor can do is press their nose against the lattice windowpane and peer enviously at the privileged world reviewed within. Like Thomas Hardy's hero, we are all obscure Judes, in awe of this world-renowned seat of learning. Here, perhaps more than in any other English city, time stands quite literally still. Whole quadrangles and cloisters seem frozen in a medieval eternity where only the undergraduates' ubiquitous bicycles break the chronological spell. From the upper deck of an open-topped tourist bus the sightseer can derive a vicarious wisdom. After all, you can now truthfully recall: "When I was at Oxford."

THE ANCHOR - adjacent Bridge 240. Suburban pub serving a wide range of ales and meals both sessions. Tel: 01865 510282.

THE TROUT - Thames-side Godstow. Famous 12th century inn idyllically located by a foaming weir. Bass ales and a wide range of food available. Tel: 01865 554485.

THE PERCH - Thames-side Binsey. Thatched riverside inn set back from the Thames behind a mask of trees. Large garden, wide menu. Tel: 01865 240386.

THE PLOUGH - adjacent Bridge 236, Wolvercote. Morrells and good food if you can find somewhere to moor!

WATERMAN'S ARMS - Thames-side above Osney Lock. Cosy Morland pub offering home-made food. Tel: 01865 248832.

LE PETIT BLANC - Walton Street. Tel: 01865 510999. Raymond Blanc owned restaurant hidden away in the backstreets of Jericho.

THE NOSEBAG - St Michael's Street. Classic wholefood restaurant/cafe. Tel: 01865 721033.

JUDE THE OBSCURE - Walton Street. Tel: 01865 553344. CAMRA recommended Jericho local within handy proximity of the canal.

FISHERS - St Clements. Close to Magdalen Bridge. Quite a stroll from the canal but well worth it, as this is Oxford's best fish and seafood restaurant, and; in any case, you'll be rewarded with the view down onto the Cherwell from Magdalen Bridge on the way. Tel: 01865 243003.

Drawing on a wide range of custom and taste - town & gown and tourists - Oxford's shops are inspired to a admirable eclecticism. The COVERED MARKET (off High Street) hosts the most wonderful cross-section of retailers - food, books, clothes and cafes - and deserves a visit, whilst bookshops, not surprisingly, are to the fore; there are several branches of Blackwells ("the world's finest bookshop") and the Oxford University Press have their own outlet in High Street.

 TOURIST INFORMATION - The Old School, Gloucester Green. Tel: 01865 726871.

WALKING TOURS - conducted tours from TIC.

GUIDE FRIDAY - open-top bus rides with commentary. Tel: 01865 790522.

THE OXFORD STORY - Broad Street. Tel: 01865 728822. Jorvik style ride through Oxford's rich history.

MUSEUM OF OXFORD - St Aldates. Open Tue-Sat, admission charge. Tel: 01865 815559.

ASHMOLEAN MUSEUM - Beaumont Street. Open Tue-Sun, admission free. Britain's oldest public museum (founded 1683) displays European, Egyptian and Near Eastern antiquities. Tel: 01865 278000.

CARFAX TOWER - Carfax. 99 steps to heaven for a grandstand view of the city of dreaming spires.

PUNT HIRE - Oxford's most traditional means of seduction can be hired from boat houses at Folly Bridge on the Thames and Magdalen Bridge on the Cherwell.

COLLEGES - over thirty colleges make up 'Oxford University'. Many of them are world famous, such as Balliol and Merton which are both of 13th century origin; Magdalen (pronounced 'Maudlin') which dates from 1458; and Christ Church founded in 1525 by Cardinal Wolsey. The general public are admitted to most of them in the afternoons.

OPEN SPACES - much of Oxford's charm rests in the proliferation of green spaces, the city's lungs. These include: The Parks, Christ Church Meadow and Port Meadow. A stroll - or a picnic - on any of them comes as a refreshing experience after the hurly burly of the main thoroughfares and helps put Oxford in the context of its riverside setting.

BUSES - local and district services provided by the Oxford Bus Company. Tel: 01865 785400.

TRAINS - services to Reading, London, Birmingham etc, plus local stations, from the station on the western edge of the city. Tel: 08457 484950.

Residential suburb situated between the canal and the Thames. Useful post office stores which also sells Calor Gas, fish & chip shop and THE PLOUGH (Tel: 01865 556969), accessed from Bridge 236, where bar and restaurant meals are served. Regular buses to/from Oxford city centre.

# The Grand Union Canal

Frosty Autumn morning at Cosgrove, Grand Union Canal

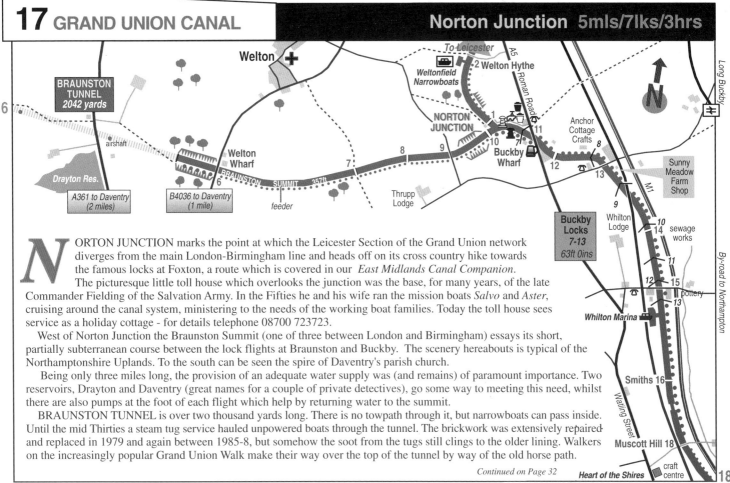

**N**ORTON JUNCTION marks the point at which the Leicester Section of the Grand Union network diverges from the main London-Birmingham line and heads off on its cross country hike towards the famous locks at Foxton, a route which is covered in our *East Midlands Canal Companion*.

The picturesque little toll house which overlooks the junction was the base, for many years, of the late Commander Fielding of the Salvation Army. In the Fifties he and his wife ran the mission boats *Salvo* and *Aster*, cruising around the canal system, ministering to the needs of the working boat families. Today the toll house sees service as a holiday cottage - for details telephone 08700 723723.

West of Norton Junction the Braunston Summit (one of three between London and Birmingham) essays its short, partially subterranean course between the lock flights at Braunston and Buckby. The scenery hereabouts is typical of the Northamptonshire Uplands. To the south can be seen the spire of Daventry's parish church.

Being only three miles long, the provision of an adequate water supply was (and remains) of paramount importance. Two reservoirs, Drayton and Daventry (great names for a couple of private detectives), go some way to meeting this need, whilst there are also pumps at the foot of each flight which help by returning water to the summit.

BRAUNSTON TUNNEL is over two thousand yards long. There is no towpath through it, but narrowboats can pass inside. Until the mid Thirties a steam tug service hauled unpowered boats through the tunnel. The brickwork was extensively repaired and replaced in 1979 and again between 1985-8, but somehow the soot from the tugs still clings to the older lining. Walkers on the increasingly popular Grand Union Walk make their way over the top of the tunnel by way of the old horse path.

*Continued on Page 32*

*Continued from Page 31*

South of Norton Junction lie BUCKBY LOCKS. Buckby is well known throughout the waterways as the home of the 'Buckby Can'. These metal water carriers, adorned with 'rose & castles', were an essential piece of the boat families' inventory, because their boats were not equipped with water tanks and running water from the tap. Watling Street crosses the canal at Buckby Wharf and here the towpath changes sides. For a couple of miles the canal is in close proximity to the M1 motorway and correspondingly loses much of its inherent peace and quiet. The ghosts in this landscape must be severely disturbed, but ghosts there must be, for the Roman settlement of Bannaventa stood adjacent to what is now Whilton Marina, and the medieval village of Muscott lay adjacent to Bridge 18.

## SUMMARY OF FACILITIES *(Map 17)*

There's only one pub remotely near the canal on Map 17 and that's the NEW INN (Tel: 01327 842540) by Buckby Top Lock. Home cooking's available to takeaway from SUNNY MEADOW FARM SHOP near Bridge 13.

Stroll up from Bridge 18 to the HEART OF THE SHIRES shopping village, a group of specialist shops (including a tea room) housed in what was a Victorian 'model' farm. Those all important holiday souvenirs may be purchased at ANCHOR COTTAGE CRAFTS (between bridges 12 and 13), WHILTON LOCKS POTTERY (Bridge 15), or at the WHILTON CHANDLERY (beside Whilton Marina), where provisions are also on sale.

TRAINS - useful staging post for towpath walkers at Long Buckby station 1 mile east of Bridge 13. Silverlink trains. Tel: 08457 484950.

Buckby Locks

WHEN Napoleon was busy acquiring as much of Europe as he could early in the 19th century, the government got out a map of England and looked for somewhere safe to hide King George III. Their eye fell upon the tiny Northamptonshire village of Weedon Bec which, not entirely coincidentally, had just been linked to London with the completion of William Jessop's Grand Junction Canal. Here they built barracks and a Royal Pavilion. A canal arm led off the main line, entering the barracks through a portcullis. It was obviously intended that Weedon would be defended to the last. Happily, Bonaparte met his match elsewhere, and the King never needed to use his splendid pavilion. But the barracks remained in use for many years and, on occasions, troops were carried by canal boat from here to troublespots and ports of embarkation.

A 15 mile pound separates the lock flights at Buckby and Stoke Bruerne. To maintain this horizontality, the canal accommodates the undulations of the countryside: wrapping itself around the sinuous valley of the upper Nene, and crossing the river by way of a high embankment at Weedon.

As the canal curves round Nether Heyford there are views in the distance of Heygates flour mill on the Nene at Bugbrooke.

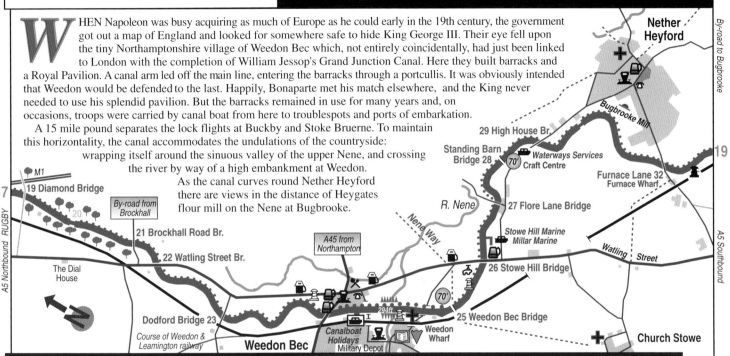

Weedon, as football cliche would have it, is a village of two halves, being divided by the canal and the railway. The quietest part lies to the west, well away from the A5, where the vast barracks may be seen, though not officially entered.

Pubs proliferate - take your pick from the HEART OF ENGLAND (Tel: 01327 340335) by Bridge 24, the PLUME OF FEATHERS (Tel: 01327 340978) in 'real' Weedon west of the canal or the CROSSROADS HOTEL (Tel: 01327 340354). A Chinese takeaway is located just along from Bridge 24, and Oriental cuisine is also

on the agenda at the NARROWBOAT (Tel: 01327 340536), beside Bridge 26, a pub whose Cantonese dishes enjoy a high reputation.

Goodness Foods have one of their health food bakeries down the road from Bridge 24, but the main village shops are located west of the canal and best reached from the offside moorings on the embankment near the church. They include two general stores, a newsagent, greengrocer, butcher and post office.

THE landscape pitches and rolls like a sea swell. One doesn't think of the Grand Union as a pretty canal - it is too businesslike and muscular for that - but its remote journeying across the Shires has the reposeful quality of a Sunday stroll. At least that's how it feels for today's pleasure boaters, doubtless the working boatmen of the past were too preoccupied with 'getting 'em ahead' to pay homage to the countryside's charm. But if the neighbouring trains emphasise the modern urge to be elsewhere, the canal acclimatizes you kindly to each new view. The passengers in Virgin's sleek air-conditioned carriages may be alighting in Euston or Glasgow before you get to Gayton, but people who go to great lengths to save time usually end up by having to kill it.

'Banbury Lane' crosses the canal at Bridge 43. Once it was a drover's road, but its origins may go back to prehistoric times. In the heyday of the canal there was a wharf and tavern here. The buildings - three storeys with an attic - are typical of the architectural style of the Grand Junction company, and similar structures can be seen at many wharves along this section of the canal. As trade evaporated, most of the canal pubs lost their licences and were converted into private residences.

At GAYTON JUNCTION the Northampton Arm branches off from the main line and commences its whirlwind descent to the Nene - turn to Map 30 for the next exciting instalment.

GAYTON JUNCTION
Turnover Br. 47

Nightingales Br. 46

By-roads from Rothersthorpe

45 Wright's Lane

44 East's Bridge

Banbury Lane 43

Evans Bridge 42

canal shop

wc

MAIN LINE

Gayton

By-road from Kislingbury & Northampton

Bugbrooke

Skew Bridge 41

Downs Lane 40

NEWS

38 Rudkins Bridge

Lover's Lane 34

35

36 70'

Bugbrooke Wharf

33

18

RUGBY

By-roads to A5 Watling Street

By-road to Blisworth

20

48

2

48

By-road from Nether Heyford

N

## BUGBROOKE

Bugbrooke boasts some immensely attractive streets of ochre coloured houses and, more prosaically, a vast working mill on the banks of the Nene at the end of a No Through Road.

THE WHARF (Tel: 01604 832585), canalside at Bridge 36, is the obvious choice in the refreshment stakes, but the BAKERS ARMS (Tel: 01604 830865) is a village 'local' of great charm where Webster's ales are normally served.

Shops include a Co-op late store, post office and general store/newsagent. A builder's merchant sells Calor Gas.

## GAYTON

A peaceful hilltop village with a fine church and two pubs, but no shops. STELLA'S CANAL SHOP at Gayton Junction sells maps, postcards, crafts and paintings, as well as a range of basic provisions.

**B**LISWORTH and Stoke Bruerne are contrasting canalside communities separated by the longest presently navigable tunnel in Britain. It takes around half an hour to pass through; time to reflect upon the tunnel's eventful history. By the time the rest of the Grand Junction Canal had opened between London and Braunston in 1800, Blisworth still wasn't finished, despite having been under construction for seven years. A temporary tramway over the top of the hill was built in its place - traces of which are still visible - and goods were laboriously shipped from boat to wagon and back again. Finally the tunnel was opened on 25th March 1805. A procession of boats journeyed through the tunnel from Blisworth, to be met at the Stoke Bruerne end by a crowd of several thousand onlookers. The procession continued down through the locks to a VIP banquet at Stony Stratford.

Blisworth Tunnel's dimensions permitted narrowboats to pass inside, but no towpath was provided. At the outset boats were poled through, rather in the manner of Oxford punts, but this practice was apparently abandoned in favour of the more traditional art of 'legging', though with, not surprisingly, a considerable number of fatalities. The canal company provided registered leggers who wore brass arm bands proclaiming their role. Later, as traffic increased, a steam tug service was provided, and

although this was withdrawn as long ago as 1936, there is still a reek and an aroma of soot and steam to be savoured within the tunnel's confines.

In the late Seventies, in common with many other impressive canal structures, BLISWORTH TUNNEL was feeling its age, and suffering from a backlog of indifferent maintenance. Its lining deteriorated to such an extent that it became necessary to close the tunnel for four years, effectively severing the canals of the Midlands from those of the South-East. Four million pounds were spent on re-lining the bore, and the tunnel re-opened, amidst much ceremony, and not a little relief amongst the boating fraternity, in August 1984.

The Grand Union skirts Blisworth, passing beneath the A43 and the West Coast Main Line in the process. This area was once riddled with iron stone quarries linked by tramway to loading stages along the canal bank, much of the stone being carried the comparatively short distance by boat to Hunsbury Hill Furnaces on the Northampton Arm (Map 30). Blisworth railway station was the junction for the Stratford & Midland Junction Railway discussed in the text accompanying Map 9 as well as the line from Blisworth to Peterborough which used to accompany much of the course of the River Nene.

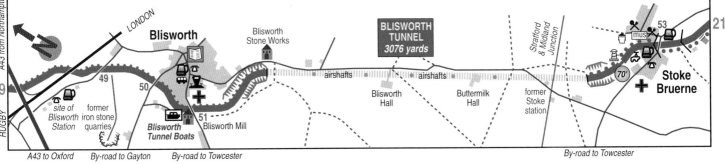

Blisworth Mill, a handsome brick building once used as a depot by the Grand Union Canal Carrying Company, overlooks Bridge 51. Blisworth Tunnel's northern portal is built from blue brick. Half an hour after entering the tunnel you can compare this with the redbrick of the southern portal. Where Blisworth dreams, Stoke Bruerne bristles; both with boaters and tourists, the latter attracted here primarily by the village's famous Canal Museum. Steerers should handle their craft with consideration and courtesy, keeping a special eye open for the trip boats which ply between the winding hole and the top lock. As the cutting recedes, the canal narrows through the site of Rectory Bridge, then widens as it reaches the wharf and associated buildings which, taken as a whole, make Stoke Bruerne such an attractive canal location.

A three-storey, stone built mill dominates the wharf. Once it ground corn with machinery driven by steam, now it houses the celebrated museum, first opened to the inquisitive public as long ago as 1963. A basin for boats delivering coal to the mill lay behind where the tall poplar trees now stand, and all trace has vanished of the roving bridge which carried the towpath over the entrance to this dock. A row of stone cottages, originally provided for millworkers, but later used by canal employees, separates the mill from a brick house of Georgian style. One of these cottages is available for holiday lettings - for details telephone 01604 862107. The Georgian house was for many years a shop catering for the needs of boating families. But in the twilight years of commercial carrying it was the home of Stoke's favourite daughter, Sister Mary Ward, a lady of high ideals and humility, who took it upon herself to look after the boat people in sickness and in health until her retirement in 1962.

As trade expanded on the Grand Junction Canal, it became necessary to duplicate the locks. Here at Stoke it is interesting to discover that the top lock in use today is the duplicate chamber, the original being on the west side of the canal and used nowadays to accommodate a boat-weighing machine from the Glamorganshire Canal and a BCN 'station boat', both being amongst the museum's outdoor exhibits; similarly the narrowboat *Sculptor* which is usually moored outside the mill unless attending a boat rally elsewhere. Buildings on the west bank of the canal include the wharfinger's office and house, now occupied by canal author, David Blagrove. Another village resident, well known in canal circles, is Brian Collings of the Guild of Waterway Artists, painter of our covers for many years.

No mooring is permitted in the lock flight at Stoke. Free 48 hour visitor moorings are available between the tunnel mouth and the museum. A 70ft winding hole is provided just south of the tunnel, and boats not proceeding south of Stoke Bruerne are advised to turn at this point. Those who do head further south should beware of the trip boats operating between the winding hole and the top lock.

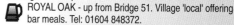

## BLISWORTH (MAP 20)

Church and chapel dominate the view from the canal, and there are some fine looking stone buildings, reminders of the village's significance as a centre of quarrying. On the road which runs across the hill in parallel to the tunnel's subterranean course, stands a handsome stone building bearing the inscription: "Blisworth Stone Works".

ROYAL OAK - up from Bridge 51. Village 'local' offering bar meals. Tel: 01604 848372.

General store and newsagent in main street of village.

BUSES - to/from Northampton & Towcester. Tel: 01604 20077.

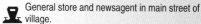

## STOKE BRUERNE (MAP 20)

Against the odds, Stoke Bruerne transcends its popularity. In high season it attracts the sort of ice cream crowds which many a theme park would be proud of. Yet it contrives to retain its integrity, remaining a tight-knit community with a mildly obsessive interest in the welfare and activity of its canal. For this is a canal village without equal, and the Grand Union runs through it like a High Street, so that for once boaters see front doors and windows rather than back.

THE BOAT INN - canalside above top lock. Expanded 'local' popular with visitors and villagers alike. Restaurant with view over canal to mill and museum. Tel: 01604 862428.
THE NAVIGATION - canalside Bridge 53. Mansfield family pub with canal-themed interior. Tel: 01604 864988.
BRUERNE'S LOCK - canalside restaurant. Tel: 01604 863654.
OLD CHAPEL - rear of museum. Tearooms, restaurant and craft shop. Tel: 01604 863284.

Even the canal's great popularity couldn't save Stoke from the loss of its village store, but milk and bread are usually obtainable at the "Boat Inn". Souvenirs etc from the CANAL SHOP beside "The Boat".

## CANAL MUSEUM

Housed in a corn mill which closed before the Great War, the museum opened in 1963, having developed from the personal collection of local lock-keeper, Jack James. Indoor exhibits include canal folk costumes, a boat cabin, an occasionally operational model of Anderton Lift, and many other fascinating, evocative and topical displays. The museum shop houses probably the best range of canal literature anywhere in the country. If you haven't a complete set of up to date Canal Companions then here's an opportunity to fill the gaps. Out of doors a preserved narrowboat is usually on view together with other bits and pieces of canal history too bulky to find a home inside. Significantly, the museum seems in no way to have been eclipsed by the establishment of the prestigious National Waterways Museum at Gloucester and we can wholeheartedly recommend it to boaters and other visitors alike.

**Open daily 10am to 5pm in Summer. Closed all day Monday in Winter and shuts at 4pm. Tel: 01604 862229.** *Admission charge.*

**The Canal Museum, Stoke Bruerne**

NORTHAMPTONSHIRE is a county more travelled through than visited. Lines of communication stretch across its hedged fields like strings across the frets on the neck of a guitar.

Perhaps that's why these roads and railways, and this canal, appear aloof from the landscape. "Sorry, can't stop," they seem to be saying: "We're just passing through."

The canal traveller spends two hours negotiating the six mile pound between Stoke Bruerne and Cosgrove: a lonely landscape characterised by ridge & furrow pasturelands. The only major landmarks are the manor house and church on the brow of the hill at Grafton, the wharf at Yardley - now enjoying a new lease of life as a boatyard - and the stark ruins of Isworth Farm by Bridge 63.

Few outside the county of Northamptonshire will claim to know the course of the River Tove, but by the time it joins the Great Ouse at Cosgrove it is a significant watercourse. It rises on the uplands east of Banbury, not far from Sulgrave Manor. At the foot of Stoke locks one arm of the river - used for private moorings - flows into the canal, whilst the other passes beneath the man made waterway. A series of overflow weirs are bridged by the towpath. South of Bozenham Mill the Tove forms the boundary with Buckinghamshire.

Stoke Locks form another step in the Grand Union's roller-coaster ride between London and Birmingham: the old Grand Junction Canal had summits at Tring and Braunston; when the route was amalgamated with the Warwick & Birmingham Canal in 1929 a third summit was added at Olton near Solihull.

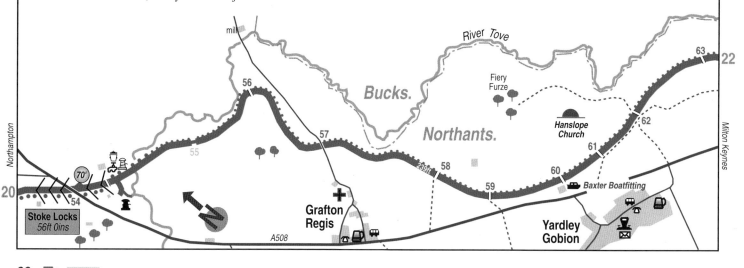

THAT old adage about the River Trent being the boundary between North and South conveniently ignores the existence of the Midlands. But here, between Cosgrove and Wolverton, the Great Ouse creates a very real sense of demarcation, separating the murky Midlands from the salubrious South; though, for a while at least, the roles seem reversed, as the canal traverses the urban sprawl of Milton Keynes to the south and the unspoilt countryside of the Tove Valley, sprinkled with stone-built villages, to the north.

High embankments prepare the canal, but not necessarily the canal traveller, for the leap across the Ouse. One moment you are on a seemingly everyday length of waterway, the next you are apparently in mid air without the benefit of a parachute. Thirty five feet below the Ouse flows unconcernedly, and all that prevents you from joining it is the narrow lip of the aqueduct's iron trough. But, unlike Pontcysyllte, these high jinks are over in a flash, and boaters really wanting to appreciate the structure should moor nearby, return on foot, and try to distinguish traces of the original locks which took the canal down to cross the river on the level, and the stone piers of the original, short-lived aqueduct.

Just above COSGROVE LOCK a short arm used as private moorings indicates the route of the former Old Stratford & Buckingham branch, a much mourned rural canal which paralleled the course of the River Ouse between here and Buckingham. It opened in 1801, measured ten miles and had two locks. But it was never much of a commercial success, being used primarily for the carriage of agricultural produce, particularly hay and straw used as fodder by London cab horses. In the event it was devoid of traffic

*Continued overleaf*

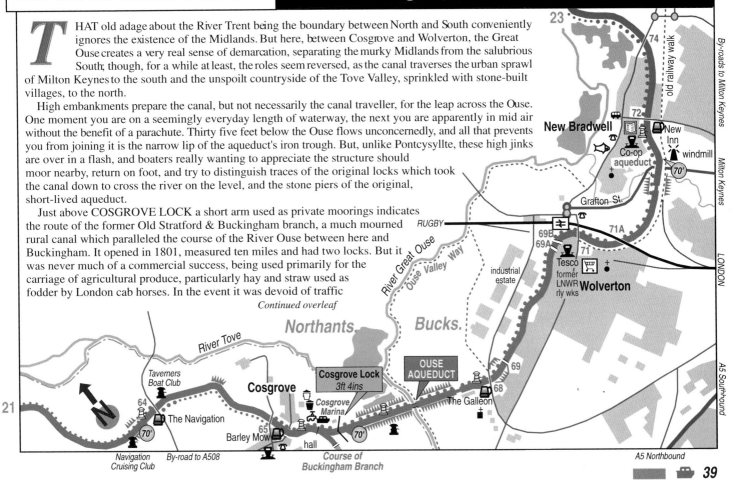

by the 1930s and officially abandoned in 1954. Attempts to have it restored were baulked when the A5 by-pass was built across its bed near Old Stratford. Perhaps the most interesting facet of its operation was the establishment of a boatbuilding yard, away from the canal itself, at Stony Stratford specialising in the construction of small sea-going vessels which had to be hauled by traction engine along the Watling Street and launched into the canal for transfer to London.

WOLVERTON, once famous for its railway works, imposes a sense of dreariness on the canal before it takes off in a broad arc around the village of NEW BRADWELL. In working boat days the boat women would hobble down the hill in their voluminous skirts to shop, catching up with their unstopping boats at the other end of the embankment. They would not recognise the huge new aqueduct carrying the canal over Grafton Street; moreover, it seems unlikely that its designers, Pell Frischman, will join Telford and Rennie in the pantheon of bridge builders. Up on the hillside the sails of a restored windmill peep over the treetops, whilst down in the valley of the Ouse flooded-out sandpits have created attractive expanses of water.

The Ouse Aqueduct, Cosgrove

## COSGROVE (MAP 22)

A quiet village away from the main road with some attractive stone buildings. On the off-side a fine row of poplar trees frames the parkland of the hall. An unusual pedestrian tunnel (once used by boat horses to reach the pub stables) passes beneath the canal, whilst Bridge 65 is unusually ornate. Sand was worked commercially down by the confluence of the Tove and Ouse. A narrow gauge railway linked the sand pits with the canal wharf and some of the rails remain in situ by the old canal junction.

THE NAVIGATION - canalside Bridge 64. Bar and restaurant food feature in this deservedly popular stone pub, together with a range of real ales. Tel: 01908 543156.

BARLEY MOW - canalside Cosgrove village. Courage and Theakston ales, bar meals both sessions and customer moorings are all available at the BM. Tel: 01908 562957.

The village's small post office stores survives and is open daily except Sundays.

## WOLVERTON (MAP 22)

A manufacturing town seemingly cast adrift from its Midlands moorings and washed aground in rural Buckinghamshire. Plenty of facilities for passing boaters: corner pubs, ethnic restaurants and fish & chips. Large TESCO store easily reached from Bridge 71; Lloyds & Barclays banks. Frequent local services from canalside station. Tel: 08457 484950.

## NEW BRADWELL (MAP 22)

A community of terraced streets built as homes for the employees of Wolverton railway works. Useful shops within a stone's throw of Bridge 72 and a nice pub, THE NEW INN (Tel: 01908 312094) offering Adnams, Wells and guest real ales as well as bar and restaurant meals and a pleasant garden. There are Chinese and Indian takeaways, too, but best of all the wonderful fish & chip shop on Newport Road, owned by second generation Italian, Luciano Pilla.

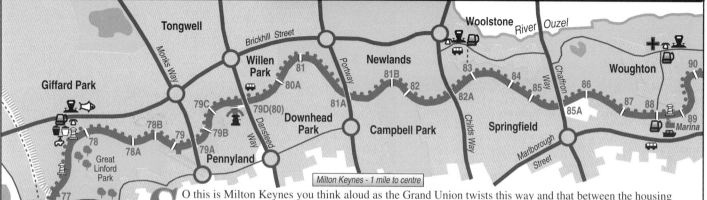

**S**O this is Milton Keynes you think aloud as the Grand Union twists this way and that between the housing developments. And how you respond is as much a matter of taste and outlook as the car you drive and the coffee you drink. The variety of architectural styles is as diverse as it is eclectic. One welcomes the good honest use of brick and timber, the refusal to be hidebound and categorised; the informality, the heterogeneity, the vernacular splashes of weatherboarding and pantiles; the canal's role as a linear park. But what comes as a surprise is the sheer un-Englishness of it all: communal drives, patios and lawns seem at odds with native Anglo-Saxon reserve, as though Milton Keynes was the blueprint for a new generation of gregarious Britons.

But, inevitably, there are disappointments. One would have welcomed more integration of houses and water; more examples of the admirable Pennyland Basin, where arms have been allowed to penetrate in and around individual dwellings, so that those inhabitants with boats can 'park' them in aquatic driveways. And the other drawback is the lack of formal visitor moorings conveniently placed for access to the city centre. Boaters need moorings in urban environments just as much as motorists need car parks, and would correspondingly be happy to pay appropriately for such facilities. A rank of secure fishbone jetties by Child's Way would encourage far more waterborne visitors to seek out the centre.

Amidst all these Brave New World developments, it is easy to forget that the canal predates the city by a century and a half. Old maps show the canal traversing a rolling landscape of scattered hamlets and the working boatmen of the past would surely be astonished at the transformation. The only canalside settlements of any note along this section were at Great Linford and Woughton on the Green. The former was notable as the point from which a branch canal led to Newport Pagnell. It had been opened in 1817 but was closed by 1846, much of its course being taken over by a branch railway, itself now converted into a pleasant public footpath.

## GREAT LINFORD (MAP 23)

Magically idyllic manorial village sympathetically encapsulated within the new city's development zone. Moor up and stroll along its neatly gravelled paths; listen to the birdsong; watch the pond life; admire the church, manor and almhouses. Pub, shop and frequent weekday bus service into Milton Keynes. THE BLACK HORSE INN - canalside Bridge 76 - is a comfortable old pub with a nice waterside garden offering bar and restaurant food. Tel: 01908 605939.

## GIFFARD PARK (MAP 23)

A new housing development of chief interest to canal users for its facilities. The GIFFARD PARK (Tel: 01908 210025) is a modern, open all day pub offering a variety of meals; it also includes a family lounge, small garden and excellent customer moorings. Across the road you'll find a post offices stores, Chinese takeaway, fish & chip shop and off licence. Buses leave at frequent intervals for the city centre.

## MILTON KEYNES (MAP 23)

When we originally encountered Milton Keynes - during compilation of the first edition of this guide back in the 1980s - it seemed so far ahead of its time and quite unlike any other British city. Now, though, its shopping malls seem all too familiar. You might be anywhere and, unless you've lots of time at your disposal, the best bet is to stay on the canal.

Family orientated 'all-day' pubs canalside by bridges 78 and 88. 'Village' locals a short walk away in Gt Linford, Woolstone and Woughton.

The main shopping area lies between Midsummer and Silbury Boulevards about one and a half miles west of the canal. Grocery markets are held on Tuesdays and Saturdays and a craft market on Thursdays.

TOURIST INFORMATION CENTRE - The Food Centre, 411 Secklow Gate East. Tel: 01908 232525. Typical tourist traps are somewhat thin on the ground in Milton Keynes, but the famous Peace Pagoda off Brickhill Street (near Bridge 81) is possibly worth a visit.

BUSES - an excellent network of 'Street Shuttles' provides easy access to/from the city centre. Tel: 01908 668366.

TRAINS - InterCity and local services from station in Central MK. Tel: 08457 484950.

**Grafton Street Aqueduct, New Bradwell**

**F**ENNY STRATFORD Lock marks the commencement of the Grand Union's climb out of the valley of the Ouse up towards the Chilterns and the summit at Tring. But, with a rise of a meagre foot, its contribution to the ascent is not impressive. In fact, it was not planned in the original survey, being built as a supposedly temporary measure to alleviate excess water pressures experienced on the long pound between here and Cosgrove. Tradition has it that southbound working boats in a hurry used to burst their way through whichever gates happened to be shut at the time, a habit the authorities would doubtless respond to with court summonses today. In any case, the lock comes as welcome exercise after the three or four hours spent glued to the tiller if you have come straight down from Cosgrove.

'Finney' marks the southern extent of Milton Keynes' sprawl. Travelling southwards it is, in many ways, reassuring to be back in the familiar world of semi-detached suburbs. Fenny Wharf was a busy spot: coal was brought to the gas works and flour and sugar carried from London Docks to Valentine's mill. As the canal emerges from its urban environment there are pleasant views across the River Ouzel and Watling Street towards the elevated heathlands of Woburn and Aspley. Northwards from Fenny Stratford the Grand Union is bordered briefly by factories before skirting the old village of Simpson on an embankment. A small aqueduct, invisible from the waterline, accommodates a footpath. There are glimpses to the east of Walton Hall, headquarters of the Open University.

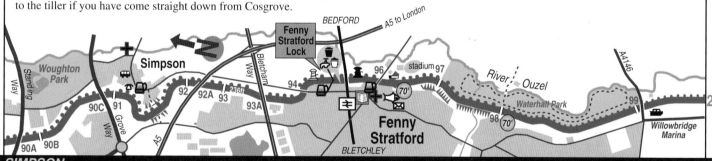

## SIMPSON

Another of Milton Keynes's antecedent villages. Buses to the city centre and a public phone. THE PLOUGH (Tel: 01908 670015) is a friendly Charles Wells pub with a garden backing on to the canal serving bar and restaurant meals.

### FENNY STRATFORD

A former coaching village on the old Watling Street, Fenny Stratford seems somewhat out on a limb and forgotten now, though there are good reasons for boaters to break their journey here, not least the provision of water, Elsan and rubbish disposal facilities.

THE BRIDGE - canalside Bridge 96. Customer moorings and bar meals. Tel: 01908 373107. CAMRA recommended. Also the RED LION adjacent to the lock. NAPOLI'S - Aylesbury Street. Italian fish & chips (and beautiful tiles) from the same family as at New Bradwell.

Not much in the way of shops in 'Finney', Bletchley being the centre of the local retailing universe.

TRAINS - Fenny Stratford's station sees sporadic trains operating between Bedford and Bletchley. Tel: 08457 484950.

THE Grand Union has probably appeared more often in canal literature than any other waterway. Classics, fictional and factual, like *The Water Gipsies, Hold on a Minute, Maiden's Trip,* and *Bread Upon the Waters,* successfully capture its atmosphere as a working waterway, but don't really prepare you for its beauty as it unravels through the Ouzel Valley, past the sandy, bracken covered hills of Linslade and over the border from Bucks to Beds. The Ouzel seems to shift some of its riverine quality upon the canal; as in all good friendships, there is a degree of exchange in character. Between bridges 109 and 111 the "Cross Bucks Way" offers towpath walkers a pretty detour above the canal past the isolated church and manor house at Old Linslade.

The Ouzel rises on Dunstable Downs and flows northwards to join the Great Ouse at Newport Pagnell. It used to be a river of many watermills, some of which survive very prettily as private dwellings. SOULBURY LOCKS - known to working boatmen as the 'Stoke Hammond Three' (which sounds more like an organ-based jazz combo) - they are overlooked by a popular pub. A picnic site and car park add to their gongoozling appeal, and if any of your crew suffer from stage fright this is not the best place for them to freeze whilst operating the locks.

The three mile pound between Soulbury and Leighton locks is captivating. Beyond the watermeadows of the Ouzel mixed woodland clothes a ridge of heathland

### Summary of Facilities

Two well known canalside pubs tempt you to pause along this length of canal. At Soulbury Locks the eponymous THREE LOCKS (Tel: 01525 272393) does a roaring trade with motorists fascinated by the activity of the locks. A wide range of meals are served and the pub is open all day in summer. Of equal popularity, THE GLOBE (Tel: 01525 373338) by Bridge 111 is a much older building, attractively weatherboarded outside and beamed within. Various real ales, bar and restaurant meals and a fine canalside patio.

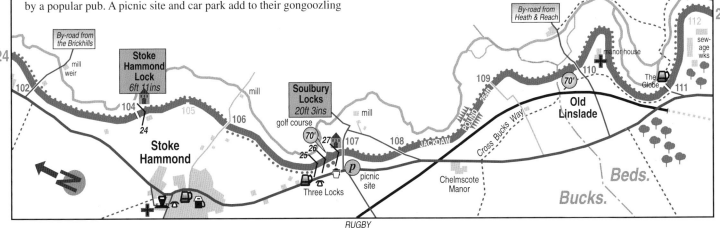

INTERRUPTED briefly - but not overwhelmed - by the shared urban environments of Linslade and Leighton Buzzard, the Grand Union Canal continues its predominantly rural progress, crossing the boundary between the counties of Bedford and Buckingham. Solitary locks come along at regular intervals, each with its own atmosphere and ambience. Leighton Lock is overlooked by a substantial, whitewashed lock-keeper's house; by Grove Lock there is a stone milepost advertising the distance to the Thames; and adjacent to Church Lock what was once the smallest chapel in Buckinghamshire has been converted into a private residence.

In the early years of the Grand Junction water shortages were experienced and, to go some way to alleviate the problem, a sequence of narrowbeam chambers were duplicated alongside the original wide locks.

These allowed single boats to use less water and also enabled the canal to cope better with its growing traffic. Remains of these locks are apparent at several locations and explain the provision of extra arches on a number of bridges. A series of pumping engines was also introduced to return water to the summit. Most of the characteristic engine houses remain. By and large they are gaunt and ghostly structures now, redolent of a time when the canal was in business to make a profit for its shareholders; though one or two have been adapted for new use. Working boatmen called them the 'Northern Engines', and naturally there were regular deliveries of coal by boat to stoke the boilers. Another local cargo was sand and there is plenty of evidence of former wharves, some still with track embedded in the towpath where narrow gauge railways ran to connect such loading points with the sand pits themselves.

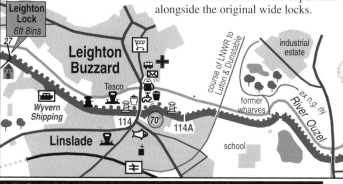

## LEIGHTON BUZZARD

An unexpectedly delightful town with a refreshing period feel; especially on Tuesdays and Saturdays when the handsome High Street throbs with the activity of a street market. A wealth of solid, provincial architecture spans the centuries - a perfect antidote to the high-tech of Milton Keynes, elevating Leighton into probably the most interesting town on the whole of the old Grand Junction.

Plenty of pubs, fish & chips and takeaways in Leighton itself, not so much choice in Linslade.

Some distinctive local shops in the town centre, notably H.G.STRATTON an award-winning butcher/baker on Market Square.
Canalside TESCO.

TRAINS - frequent Silver Link services along the Northampton-Milton Keynes -Berkhamsted corridor - useful for one way towpath walks. Tel: 08457 484950.

**S**AND gives way to clay, and clay to chalk, as the canal begins to take seriously the need to climb up to The Chilterns. Locks occur more frequently, and there is little point in those responsible for working them reboarding the boat in the intervening pounds. In any case it's fun to tramp along the towpath for a change, gazing eastwards to the furzy escarpment of the Dunstable Downs where, on a clear day, you can make out the chalk lion of Whipsnade and watch gliders making the most of upwardly mobile thermals above the rounded rampart of Ivinghoe Beacon. A mile and a half south-east of Bridge 123 is Ivinghoe and its National Trust windmill.

A sense of remoteness settles over the countryside. The boat people knew this stretch of canal as "The Fields", a typically simple yet eloquent description. The isolation is underlined when you recall that the Great Train Robbery took place on the lonely section of line north of Cheddington station in 1963.

The Grand Junction was a canal obsessed with time. Everything was date-stamped: lock chambers, bridges, tie bars, mooring rings, paddle gear. You are tempted to indulge in a sort of Victorian parlour game in which you must attach an important event to each date you come across.

Boating is brisk by Cooks Wharf where the Dunstable & District Boat Club have extensive moorings. Round the corner, tucked in between the road and railway bridges, is Grebe Canal Cruises' busy boatyard from where trip and day boats operate.

## CHEDDINGTON

This straggling commuter village, noted for fruit growing, can be reached by road from Horton and Cooks wharves, or by lane and path from Ivinghoe Locks.

OLD SWAN - quaint, thatched pub south of village centre best reached from Bridge 126. Tel: 01296 668226.
DUKE OF WELLINGTON - Cooks Wharf (reached to south of Bridge 126). Marston's ales and bar meals daily. Tel: 01296 661412.

General store and post office in village centre.

TRAINS - isolated station (from which there are views of Mentmore once the country seat of the Rothschilds but now the centre of a religious cult) served by trains between Milton Keynes and London Euston, forming a useful staging post between Leighton Buzzard and Tring for the benefit of towpath walkers. Tel: 08457 484950.

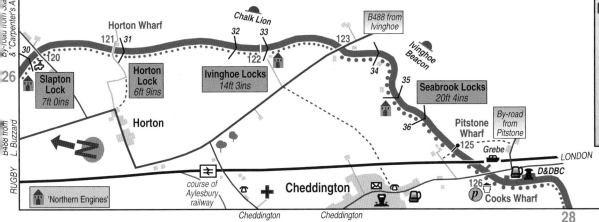

**MARSWORTH** - or, in the patois of the working boatman, "Maffers" - is a key location on the old Grand Junction's route between London and Braunston. Here the canal drops from its Tring Summit and, in doing so, crosses the boundary between Hertfordshire and Buckinghamshire. Seven wide locks used up their fair share of water and, as traffic grew, a series of reservoirs were constructed to keep the canal in water. The Upper and Lower courses of the prehistoric Icknield Way (now known as the B488 and B489 respectively) cross the canal at either extremity of the flight. The road connected East Anglia with Salisbury Plain. A delightful account of its course was written by Edward Thomas - perhaps better known as a poet than a topographical writer - and published in 1916, a year before he was killed at the Battle of Arras. His text, however, pays scant attention to the canal, other than to remark on a certain 'foreign' character

created by the setting of the reservoirs. From MARSWORTH JUNCTION (overlooked by British Waterways' office and maintenance depot) the Aylesbury Arm commences its lovely journey down to the county town of Buckinghamshire. Its course is fully described in the text accompanying Map 29.

BULBOURNE JUNCTION lies immediately above the top chamber of the Marsworth flight. It forms an attractive canalscape, a covered drydock and a junction house providing particularly graceful features. The Wendover Arm brings a welcome supply of water into the main line. The six mile branch was built primarily with this role in mind, though a flour mill and the famous boatbuilding yard of Bushell Bros. brought extra activity. Seepage caused abandonment of the central section of the arm in 1904, but it is still feasible to navigate as far as Tringford, where what looks like a winding hole capable of handling up to sixty feet of boat is available. It's a detour well worth making. Freshly pumped up from

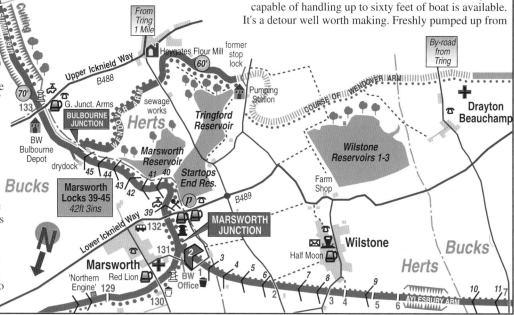

the reservoirs, the water is decidedly clear; clear enough to spy giant pike basking in the prolific weed. Progress by boat is necessarily slow, but soon the firsta overbridge appears and, immediately beyond it, a large and flourishing flour mill. It was here, where Heygates park their lorries now, that Bushells had their boatyard. Beyond the mill comes the winding hole and then perhaps another quarter of a mile of canal in water. Tringford pumping station stands adjacent to a former stop lock, west of which the canal bed is dry, though the towpath is comfortably walkable all the way to Wendover. Formed in 1989, the Wendover Arm Trust aims to restore navigation back to Wendover. An information box containing leaflets about both the Arm and the Trust's activities is located at BULBOURNE JUNCTION; it may be opened with a standard BW key.

Just south of the junction stand the elegant Bulbourne workshops. The principal activity here is the manufacture of lock gates and you may well glimpse some of the vast timbers involved in the process lying in or around the yard. Beyond the depot the canal passes beneath the Upper Icknield Way and enters TRING CUTTING. Stretching for one and a half miles, and reaching a maximum depth of thirty feet, the cutting is said to have taken the best part of five years to dig. With equipment no more sophisticated than pick-axes and wheel-barrows, this is not a surprising statistic. But the labour of two centuries ago seems nebulous now. Nature long ago reclaimed the gash in her side, soothed it with vegetation, and created a chasm of narcotic splendour. For an absolute contrast, take the lane which crosses turnover Bridge 134 and walk eastwards to view the parallel railway cutting engineered by Robert Stephenson, an altogether more ambitious affair - as befits its time - and one still disturbed by the frequent passage of trains upon its four tracks.

## MARSWORTH (Map 28)

A quiet, unassuming village on the border of Bucks and Herts, dominated by a nice flint-towered church. Three pubs and a tea room but *no* shops!

RED LION - adjacent Bridge 130. Classic village pub long favoured by canal travellers. Buckinghamshire brewed Vale beers feature; comfortable sofas, comforting food ordered at the kitchen door. Tel: 01296 668366.
WHITE LION (Tel: 01442 822325) by Bridge 132.
ANGLERS RETREAT (Tel: 01422 822250), down the road from Bridge 132. Or try BLUEBELL'S TEAROOMS (and craft shop) by Lock 39.
BUSES - regular Aylesbury-Dunstable service. Tel: 01296 84919.

## BULBOURNE (Map 28)

No shops, but the GRAND JUNCTION ARMS (Tel: 01442 890677) by Bridge 133 is a popular pub with a large garden. Bar meals served most days. Customer moorings.

## WILSTONE (Map 28)

Small village alongside the Aylesbury Arm. Little pub called the HALF MOON - all beams and gleaming brass - Tel: 01442 826410, as well as a well-stocked village store, antique shop, and farm shop on B489.

## AYLESBURY (MAP 29)

In spite of its status as the county town of Buckinghamshire, Aylesbury is a comparatively small place. It became an administrative centre when Buckingham was partially destroyed by fire in 1725. One's first impressions are tainted by a surfeit of glass, concrete and traffic. But somehow the old heart of the town survives, grouped about the market place with its cobbles, statues, clocktower and handsome municipal buildings. Deeper into the town, along attractive lanes and alleyways, and you come upon the substantial parish church of St Mary's - the highest and probably the most peaceful point in Aylesbury.

THE SHIP - cosy little street corner pub backing on to the basin, serving bar lunches (not Suns). Tel: 01296 421888.
BELL HOTEL - Market Square. Dignified hotel where bar and restaurant meals are available. Tel: 01296 89835.

The town centre is a five minute walk from the canal basin. Two indoor precincts are occupied by most household names. JACKSONS the bakers seem to pop up everywhere but canal folk don't have far to go because the bakery backs onto the basin: nice cream cakes for those who've just lock-wheeled down from Marsworth.
TOURIST INFORMATION CENTRE - Bourbon Street. Tel: 01296 330559.
BUCKINGHAMSHIRE COUNTY MUSEUM - Church Street. Admission free. Everything you always wanted to know about Bucks. Tel: 01296 331441.
BUSES - services throughout the area. Tel: 0345 382000.
TRAINS - services to/from London Marylebone. Tel: 0345 484950.

Locking down the Aylesbury Arm

49

*To Brentford & The Thames*

TRING'S three mile summit section extends from Bulbourne to Cowroast. As the canal emerges from Tring Cutting there are views eastwards above the beechwoods to the urn-topped column which stands on Aldbury Common, about a mile and a half east of Tring railway station. The monument was erected in 1832 in memory of the doyen of canal promoters, Francis Egerton, the third Duke of Bridgewater. The neighbouring estate of Ashridge House was one of the 'Canal Duke's' properties, albeit one that he allowed to fall into ruin. Inside the column a staircase climbs to a viewing balcony two hundred feet above the ground. Owned now by the National Trust, it is open to the public on summer weekends.

In contrast to the graceful splendour of the Duke's monument and its sylvan setting, the opposite bank of the canal is occupied by a 'Buffer Depot', a semi-secret government establishment used for the storage of supplies held pending a national emergency. This one abuts a well-piled wharf, suggesting that the Civil Service has more faith in the Grand Union's capacity for commercial trade than British Waterways.

COWROAST is a popular boating centre, a lagoon providing moorings for private craft off the main line. The lock here is picturesque and well cared for. Look out for the pump house, the cast-iron span of Bridge 137 (protected by lozenge-shaped weight restriction notices) and the former Control Office responsible for correlating boat movements up and down the Grand Union in carrying days.

South of Cowroast the 'Grand Junction' commences its journey down to the Thames at Brentford. A steady procession of locks takes the canal along the valley of the little River Bulbourne. Tennis courts, recreation grounds and a non-league football stadium herald the approach to BERKHAMSTED, a civilised town which clearly takes a pride in the appearance of its canal and, by the same token, creates a favourable impression with canal travellers be they on foot or afloat. Graffiti and vandalism are conspicuously absent as the canal moves agreeably along its corridor between the railway and the A4251. A totem pole beside a new housing development and an immaculately kept boatyard add interest and incident to the journey - where else could you be but among the Golden Tribes of the sunny South-East of England?

castle

142    55
*Bridgewater Boats*

**Berkhamsted Locks 53-55**
*16ft 10ins*

53

Berkhamsted Town F.C.

**Berkhamsted**

52
("Gas Two")

51

A416 to Amersham

140

B4506 from Dunstable

("Bushes") 50    Sports Centre

Tunnel

Northchurch Common

49    139

**Northchurch Locks 49-52**
*27ft 0ins*

River Bulbourne    **Northchurch**

138

By-road from Aldbury

**Bridgewater Monument**

RUGBY

Cowroast Lock
*6ft 0ins*

Cowroast Marina

48    **Dudswell**

47

**Dudswell Locks 47 & 48**
*13ft 4ins*

TRING SUMMIT    136    46    137    70'    **Cowroast**

39¼ft

28    Buffer Depot

A4251 to Aylesbury

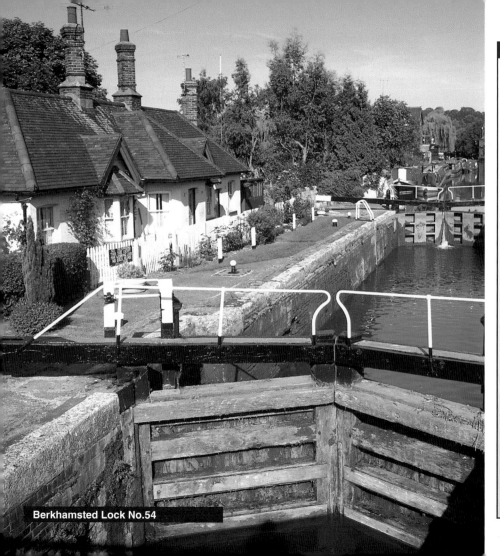

Berkhamsted Lock No.54

## BERKHAMSTED

Now by-passed by the A41, Berkhamsted belongs once again to its inhabitants (and passing canal travellers); its traffic-calmed main thoroughfare is a pleasant place to saunter, window-shopping or just 'promenading' on warm summer evenings. The town's best buildings are its oldest: the flint built parish church of St Peter and the ruined Norman castle, once the residence of the Black Prince.

Three canalside pubs of contrasting character vie for your custom: there's the CRYSTAL PALACE by Bridge 141 (Tel: 01442 862998); THE BOAT by Bridge 142 (Tel: 01442 877152), an excellent Fullers pub well regarded for its food and the RISING SUN (Tel: 01442 864913), an unspoilt Benskins house overlooking Lock 55. But if you head in to the town centre, then a host of excellent restaurants await your culinary pleasure - take your pick from Italian, Chinese, Thai etc.

Berkhamsted's little shops are full of character and include a first class butchers called EASTWOODS within a chop's throw of the canal at Bridge 142. Other interesting outlets include a fishmongers and delicatessen. If you so desire, you may patronise Tesco or Waitrose, the latter being the closest to the canal. All the main high street banks have branches in the town centre - all, in the words of a recent advertising slogan, just waiting to help you live your life.

TRAINS - frequent local trains between London Euston, Milton Keynes and Northampton, calling at Tring, Cheddington and Leighton Buzzard specifically, perhaps, for the benefit of towpath walkers. Tel: 08457 484950.

## COWROAST

Nothing to do with bovine barbecues, but a corruption of 'cow rest', a throwback to cattle droving days. The COW ROAST inn (Tel: 01442 822287) predates the canal and serves bar and restaurant meals.

51

# 29 GUC AYLESBURY ARM

ylesbury 4mls/5lks/2hrs

**Aylesbury**

Aylesbury Basin

Town Centre

industrial estate

Aylesbury Locks

By-road to Bierton

Broughton Lock

Red House Lock

Buckland Lock

**Herts.** **Bucks.**

I
N common with the Northampton Arm, the Aylesbury Arm has the dubious distinction of featuring a considerable number of locks in a comparatively short distance. But the Aylesbury Arm's attraction lies not so much in the steepness of the gradient as in the tranquillity of its setting. Once you have negotiated the staircase lock at Marsworth (Map 28) you are ravished by the immediate and utter intimacy of the arm, which proceeds to spill down into the Vale like an apple-cart rumbling along a country lane. In fields bordering the canal, pigs frolic in the mud and hens scrat for tasty morsels on a dung heap. For a couple of miles the arm passes into Hertfordshire, but the landscape remains aloof, the inherent peace of the canal being broken only by the hooting of car horns as they approach each hump-backed bridge.

At this point you will probably be impatient for facts, even though, as Sir John Squire once ruefully pointed out, they are only flies in the amber. But the bare essentials are that the canal was promoted late in the 18th century as a through route across the Vale of Aylesbury to the Thames at Abingdon, from whence connection could be made via the Wilts & Berks and Kennet & Avon canals to Bath and Bristol. What a mouth-watering canal odyssey that would have made possible. However, only the arm to Aylesbury materialised and, following its opening in 1815, it settled down to a century and a half of trade, notably to and from Nestles condensed milk factory near the terminus of the arm and through the carrying activities of the well known boat company Harvey-Taylor.

Although the Aylesbury Arm is essentially a rural canal there is much to see and discuss. As you proceed across the border into Herts there are views to the north of Mentmore, designed by Paxton for one of the Rothchilds but more recently occupied by Transcendentalists. Soon the flint tower of Marsworth church is left astern and, as the gradient eases, the locks come less closely spaced.

Red House Lock is named after an isolated inn of the same name which stood alongside it, but which was converted into a private residence in the mid Sixties. Beyond here the channel narrows perceptibly and the reeds seem to whisper like conspirators as you pass. Presently the outskirts of Aylesbury make their presence felt and, as if to emphasise this, locks 14 and 15 are fitted with anti-vandal handcuff locks. Industry then takes over, notably Nestles whose plant once provided so much trade for the canal. Two demure lines of terraced houses, linked by a footbridge, herald the L-shaped terminal basin with its friendly community of residential boats. You may even be welcomed by a member of the local canal society and pointed politely to a suitable mooring in the shadow of the Inland Revenue office block which dominates the basin. Relax, overnight moorings are tax deductible.

*Details of Aylesbury and its facilities appear on page 48.*

**52**

# The River Nene

**Ashton Lock, near Oundle, on the River Nene**

From Gayton

19

Gayton Marina
(Alvechurch)

1

3

4

5

5

6

A43

Rothersthorpe
Locks 1-13
77ft 6ins

11 12
M1

8

13

Swan Valley
Industrial Est.

services

9

10

11

Wootton
Lock 14

St Crispin's
Hospital
Tower

12

A45

Duston Mill

13

Hardingstone Lock 15

Six Fields
Leisure

Northampton
Town F.C.

Hunsbury Hill
Country Park

site of
ironworks

River Nene

Nene Way

Express
Lifts Tower

A428 to Rugby

RUGBY   A508 to Market Harborough

14

Hunsbury Lock 16

maltings

Retail Park

gas works

KFC

West Bridge

50'

Carlsberg
Brewery

corn merchants

Northampton
Lock 17

South Bridge

Market
Square

Guildhall

Delapre
Abbey

Midland
Railway
warehouse

Avon

Morrison

Becket's Park

wc

Town Lock

former
power
station

Northampton

31

**Locking down the Northampton Arm**

THE Northampton Arm presides over the canal travellers' access to the River Nene like an intimidating security guard, its seventeen narrowbeam locks seemingly set in a daunting scowl calculated to deter all but the most obstinate boater from making the descent to Northampton and the river. Nor is the arm quite the rural backwater it once was. Northampton's burgeoning retail parks, housing estates and business centres are rapidly erasing the watermeadow landscape which once characterised the arm's entrance to the county town. And yet (and how often canals throw up an unexpected "and yet") the three or four hours spent navigating the arm are full of interest and entertainment. And in a way the effort required to operate all those locks is a cloud with a silver lining because, after the arm, even the Nene's notoriously arduous guillotine gates seem comparatively easy going in comparison.

We set off down the arm from Gayton at six on an August morning already hinting at autumn. Mist lay cupped in the fields and spiders' looms were frozen on the lock gear. But the day which had started with a woollen jumper nip in the air was resorting to tee-shirts by the time we locked down on to the Nene at nine o'clock. The locks posed no undue problems, other than a certain frustration that the positioning of the guard rails on the tail mitred pairs made crossing from one to another diffcult. Nevertheless, with two eleven year olds and a forty-something on lock duty, we averaged six minutes per lock without any undue sense of hurry.

Bridges 5 and 8 are picturesque timber affairs, seemingly padlocked open. The canal passes beneath the M1 by way of a concrete vault, built in 1959, and for a decade or so this crossing regularly presented the piquant contrast of horse-drawn butty boats making their stately progress beneath the hurtling road traffic. Below Lock 13, the A43, following the course of the one time Blisworth, Northampton & Peterborough railway (the Nene Valley line which accompanies the river for much of its course) veers away from the canal and, briefly, the canal regains some of its rural character: not a bad spot to moor if you've come down the flight of an evening and haven't the energy or daylight left to proceed any further.

At Bridge 12 Northampton begins to fill the skyline. To the north-west the tower of St Crispin's Hospital dominates the ridge, but as vertical landmarks go it is outdone by Express Life's 418ft high test tower, known locally as Northampton's 'lighthouse'. The Queen opened it in 1982 and it is used for testing high speed lifts. If your heart plummets just as rapidly at the thought of that, turn your attention to the past where, by Hardingstone Lock, between 1873 and 1921 stood the extensive premises of Hunsbury Hill Ironworks. A considerable volume of iron ore came down by boat to the works from the quarries at Blisworth.

The canal's entrance into Northampton is less than salubrious. The award-winning but legobrick-like architecture of the Carlsberg Brewery makes the Scandinavian influence doubly apparent, and though it can be argued that this in itself makes a positive contribution to the environment, the general effect is somewhat seedy, Lock 17 being ensconsed in a subcontinent of builders merchants yards, crane-hire depots and container parks. So it comes as a relief to lock into the river, at which point diehards might be tempted into exploring the short Westbridge Arm long ago used by boats trading to and from the gasworks and a number of other local wharves. Shallow, weedy and limited to boats of fifty feet and less by the confines of the winding hole at its end, this backwater is one of those obscure little waterways with which connoisseurs of canal travel seek to surpass their peers. Most boaters, however, will be content to go with the flow and navigate beneath the stately South Bridge, beyond which, on the towpath side, a line of bollards overlooked by a row of not unpleasing modern flats, provides Northampton's best mooring facility. Mooring used to be recommended alongside Becket's Park, but this is now, during darkness at least, reputedly the haunt of undesirables, though the Borough Council are believed to be looking into ways of rectifying the situation. How sad it is that mooring in urban areas almost invariably involves making a benefit versus risk calculation. It wasn't like that in yesteryear.

Town Lock is the first river lock that eastbound travellers encounter. It is not typical because its tail gates are a mitred pair and not the guillotine-type gate normally associated with the river. It is, however, of wide beam dimensions, emphasising the restrictive nature of the Northampton Arm and its narrow beam locks which prevented through trading of broad craft between the Grand Union and the waterways of East Anglia.

## NORTHAMPTON (Map 30)

We liked Northampton immensely, stopping on both our downstream and upstream journeys to visit the Saturday market. On both occasions we moored by the new flats between South Bridge and Town Lock, strolling into the town centre by way of the cattle market (since sadly replaced by a supermarket) where auctioneering was going full pelt. Within ten minutes we were in the town centre with its thriving and spacious market place, the first time missing Ben Elton by minutes, he being due to do a signing session at Dillons bookstore. "What are we going to do in Northampton?" wailed the eleven year olds, but returned from half an hour's freedom from grown-ups with enthusiasm for the shops and market stalls. Returning by road for some hard core research, we had time at our disposal to discover some of Northampton's wonderful, yet largely unsung, architecture. Tucked away unselfconsciously on Derngate is the house (No.78) which Charles Rennie Mackintosh designed for the model-maker Bassett Lowke, but there are no plaques to recall this and it is not open to the public. Much more bullish is the Guildhall on St Giles Square, a Victorian Gothic edifice dating from 1864. Nearby stands All Saints, a fine 17th century church rebuilt following the town's catastrophic fire of 1675: John Clare is remembered within.

FISH INN - Fish Street. Atmospheric town centre pub with wide choice of real ales.

THE BEAMHOUSE - Fish Street. Mansfield Brewery refurbishment.

WIG & PEN - St Giles Street. Good for lunches.

LUIGI'S VINEYARD - Italian Restaurant at the town centre end of Derngate. Bookings on 01604 33978.

ACME DINER - Fish Street. American style eating house.

BRITANNIA INN - riverside below Rush Mills Lock. Likeable family-style pub offering food and customer moorings. Nice playground for children.

Northampton is rightly renowned for its imposing, 13th century market square, said to be the second largest in England. Over two hundred stalls squeeze into the square on Tuesdays, Wednesdays, Fridays and Saturdays. In contrast the Grosvenor Centre is a typical modern mall housing all the well-known chain stores: comfortably familiar yet you could be anywhere. Other worthwhile shopping zones include Peacock Place and Abington Street.

TOURIST INFORMATION - St Giles Square. Tel: 01604 22677.

MUSEUM & ART GALLERY - Guildhall Road. The largest display of boots and shoes in the world etc. etc. Tel: 01604 39415.

COUNTRYSIDE CENTRE - Guildhall Road. Tel: 01604 237220. Shop and information centre devoted to Northamptonshire's countryside and local crafts.

BUSES - United Counties/Stagecoach. Tel: 01604 702112.

TRAINS - Silver Link services. Tel: 08457 484950.

## BILLING (Map 31)

Great & Little Billing themselves lie beyond the A45's dual carriageways and are thus largely irrelevant to boaters and walkers along the Nene Way. Riverside Billing is dominated by the Aquadrome, 235 acres of parkland and lakes offering numerous leisure facilities and seasonal holiday home hire. Tel: 01604 408181.

BUGLASS GALLERY COFFEE SHOP - adjacent Clifford Hill Lock. Charming little eatery adjunct to decorative metal craft shop.

BILLING MILL - adjacent Billing Lock. Mansfield Brewery restaurant/pub ("informal dining for all the family") housed in sympathetically restored watermill, well worth visiting even if you normally steer clear of such establishments. The wheel still turns and there's an evocative display of watermill photographs.

## COGENHOE (Map 31)

Pronounced 'Cook-no', the village centre lies a ten minute uphill walk from the lock. Infills of modern housing have rendered the village less visually attractive than it might otherwise have been, but the 13th century church is worth visiting.

ROYAL OAK - village centre. Not the most prepossesing of Nene pubs (from the outside at any rate) but undeniably one of the friendliest and the bar food is both nourishingly tasty and inexpensive. Beer on draught includes Everards from Leicester and Marstons from you know where.

Newsagent and general store in the village but also a moderate selection of provisions etc available from caravan site shop adjacent to lock.

## EARLS BARTON (Map 32)

Shoe-making village notable for its Saxon-towered church dating from 970. This is readily visible from the river, but the village is a bit of a hike from White Mills Lock. One of our crew was determined to make a pilgrimage to this architectural treasure, whose significance had been drilled into him by an enthusiastic art teacher twenty-five years earlier, but was out-voted by the Philistines. So he returned by road and spent an enraptured half hour in the church's cool interior. Had he known that Bakers Shoes had a factory shop in Earls Barton he might have had more success in tempting the crew to follow in his footsteps. There is also a small museum devoted to local life, though this is only open on Saturdays.

NORTHAMPTON'S eastern outskirts are not as decrepit as those to the west. Running alongside the idyllically named Midsummer Meadow, the navigation channel pursues a course dating from the 1979 Washlands Scheme. The old chimney on the north bank remains from a former sewage works. The river is wide and old maps show the existence of 'bathing sheds' on its banks, suggesting that there was a time when swimming in the Nene was officially sanctioned and encouraged. In the distance, beyond the Bedford Road, stands St Andrews Hospital where John Clare, the poet, was incarcerated. On the meadows south of the river, now filled with electricity pylons and the remains of the old railways to Bedford and Peterborough, the Battle of Northampton was fought out during the Wars of the Roses in 1460.

How good it feels to have living water beneath you, subject to fluctuating currents and moods, though paradoxically the next stretch of the navigation has a definite canal feel to it. Passing under the A45 the river splits into two, the wider flood channel heading off northwards, the navigation channel more intimately twisting towards the lock at RUSH MILLS overlooked by a business park. Rush Mill Lock has mitred gates top and bottom as does Abington. Between the two the "Britannia Inn" offers limited customer moorings and the opportunity for a break of journey. Below ABINGTON LOCK you pass under a barrage gate and rejoin the main river along a wide reach on which mooring is prohibited. Halfway along here a sluice controls access into and out of a floodwater storage reservoir with a capacity of 500 million gallons. The original navigable course lay to the north of the A45 where the remains of the old Abington lock can still be discerned.

A tight bend to the north leads to another barrage gate, then you reach WESTON FAVELL LOCK, the first (going downstream) to feature a guillotine bottom gate of the style so synonymous with the Nene. This one is electrically operated, delaying your first experience of the notoriously muscle-breaking windlass-operated guillotines. Passing Northampton Boat Club's busy moorings, the river negotiates a pretty reach bounded by lofty willows before encountering CLIFFORD HILL LOCK, overlooked by a high circular mound whose historic purpose is something of a mystery, though it was manifestly erected to guard over a ford in the river. Alongside the lock chamber is a grave-like stone commemorating Spencer Compton, a local MP, who, in an early example of industrial sponsorship, paid for the construction of the lock around 1760.

Billing Aquadrome, a caravan, camping and amusement centre developed in the Twenties on the site of gravel workings, dominates the next three quarters of a mile. The locks attract crowds of onlookers and you are expected to do interviews, pose for photographs and kiss the babies. One of the flooded gravel pits has been adapted as a marina, access being by way of a tightish bend by Billing Bridge.

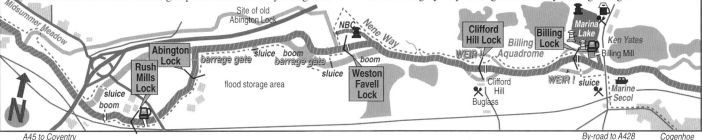

THERE are those who will tell you that the Nene (pronounced 'Nen' hereabouts) doesn't really become beautiful until it passes Wellingborough, or even Thrapston. But we found the river in the neighbourhood of Earls Barton comely enough, traversing its wide flood, gravel-pit-riddled plain and punctuated, every mile or so, by locks readily visible from a distance on account of the high guillotine gates at their tails. You become accustomed to the layout of these locks, their operation and their idiosyncrasies. The spindle on the guillotine has to be accessed first with a river authority key (obtainable at Gayton Marina if you are new to the river). Other points to bear in mind include using side fenders to prevent your boat snagging the prominent mooring chain bolts on the lock walls and, on a less serious level, ducking to avoid drips down your neck when passing under the vertical gate. Most importantly raise the vertical gate slowly - a couple of turns are quite enough to start the water falling! We strongly urge you to acquire a copy of the Environment Agency's "Navigations in the Anglian Region" booklet before cruising on the Nene.

COGENHOE (say 'Cook-no' for maximum effect with the locals) is generally regarded as the first really attractive overnight mooring point downstream of Northampton. We tried it one night and found it most congenial; but, in fact, most of the lock cuts along this stretch offer informal moorings if you are not averse to sharing the bankside with cattle and sheep.

WHITE MILLS LOCK is another pleasant mooring from which, perhaps with the aid of bicycles, there is access to Earls Barton (1 mile) with its wonderful Saxon church, or Castle Ashby (2 miles) where the parkland was landscaped by Capability Brown.

DODDINGTON LOCK is overlooked by Hardwater Mill whose origins are too far back in history for anyone to have dated. Thomas a Becket is said to have hidden here after escaping from Northampton Castle in 1164 and there is record of a 14th century miller who drowned. Now a private residence, the owner, something of a cat lover, leaves a visitors' book by the lock for passers-by to sign.

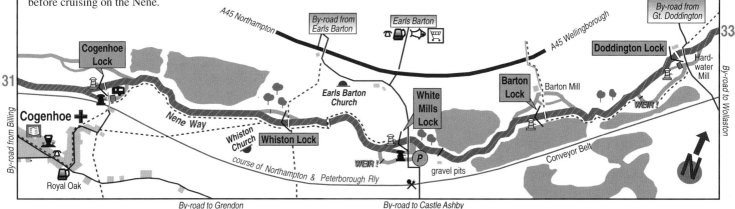

WELLINGBOROUGH imposes a temporary sense of urbanisation on the Nene, though this barely ruffles the river's inherent calm, the main images you retain being the local prison on its hillside overlooking Upper Wellingborough Lock and Whitworths' massive flour mill. This mill was the destination of the Nene's last commercial traffic in the shape of wheat imported through London Docks and carried to Wellingborough by narrowboat via Northampton until 1969. The mill - still very definitely in business - overlooks a little park which provides pleasant moorings, though local boaters (who are invariably friendly and helpful towards visitors) tend to advise against stopping here overnight. Water is laid on, however, and the park's waste bins are capacious enough to accommodate most of the average boater's accumulated rubbish.

LOWER WELLINGBOROUGH LOCK has steel piled sides with a concrete capping. Horizontal balks of timber run along the full length of the lock on both sides and, even with fenders lowered, it is necessary to exercise great care to avoid being 'hung up' on these timber balks.

Having risen at Naseby in Leicestershire, on the same watershed which is the source of the Warwickshire Avon, the little River Ise enters the Nene above Lower Wellingborough Lock which only became a lock following the improvements of the 1930s, previously it would have been a simple staunch. An enjoyable series of hairpin bends lies upstream of twin viaducts carrying the old Midland main line on its way from Leicester to London St Pancras. Just south of the viaducts lay Irchester Junction, egress point of the Higham Ferrers branch. Roman remains have been discovered south of the river near here with every probability that there was a town beside the river and a bridge across it. A Roman soldier is said to appear from time to time as dusk falls by Chester House. This stretch is popular with anglers who seem more kindly disposed towards boaters than their canal counterparts. Perhaps this reflects the comparative dearth of boats on the Nene when compared to the Grand Union and other canals.

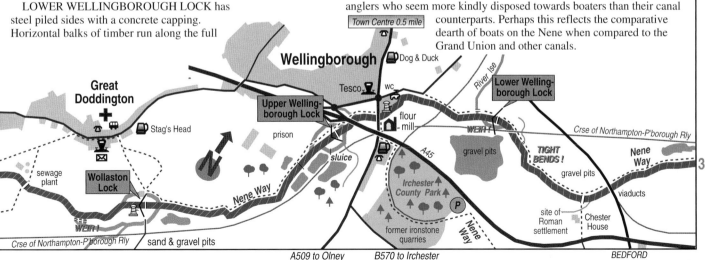

Boathouse & Lily pads, River Nene

## WELLINGBOROUGH (MAP 33)

A nondescript, South Midland town with a history of iron-working and shoe-making, Wellingborough's centre is a bleak, uninspiring trudge from the riverbank. However, as mooring overnight is not endorsed as a good idea by local boaters, the most useful facility is likely to be Tesco's supermarket, handily close to the Nene.

DOG & DUCK - London Road. Beefeater restaurant/pub 5 minutes walk from river. TESCO - adjacent riverbank by Wellingborough Bridge. All day cafe/restaurant.

## GT DODDINGTON (MAP 33)

Pleasant village reached by footpaths from Wollaston Lock. Facilities include a nice village store/delicatessen/newsagency, a small post office and the STAG'S HEAD, a convivial country pub offering both bar and restaurant food.

## IRTHLINGBORO' (MAP 34)

It's a pity that it's Irthlingborough and not Higham Ferrers, much the prettier town, which is readily accessible from the Nene. Irthlingborough is a lacklustre little town leavened only by the charm of the unusually-towered St Peter's church.

Fish & chips plus Indian and Chinese restaurants provide the basis of Irthlingborough's culinary pretensions.

The biggest store is a KwikSave supermarket. Other outlets include a butcher, baker, newsagent and chemist. There is also a small branch of the HSBC Bank.

BUSES - links with Northampton and Wellingborough provide useful staging points for Nene Way walkers. Tel: 01604 702112.

**O**NLY three locks along this length of the river, and it's difficult not to feel grateful for their relative sparsity. DITCHFORD LOCK is unusual in that its bottom gate is not a guillotine but a radial which you wind up or down in a graceful arc.

Upstream of Ditchford Lock the river is bounded by gravel workings and spanned by a bridge which sags alarmingly when the heavy gravel lorries pound across it. Another of your senses is assaulted by the proximity of a pongy offal works (euphemistically referred to as a 'sterilisation & recycling unit') and sewage plant. Below the lock a sudden intimacy is established by overhanging willows and high banks of bindweed, willowherb, osiers and nettles. Keep your eyes peeled for a glimpse of the pygmy tribe who made their home in this Amazonian landscape in 1956 after escaping from a travelling circus. At night they are said to sit at their campfire singing Alma Cogan songs, this being the last musical reference point heard whilst in captivity.

You make your own escape from the 'jungle' only to be confronted with the dual-carriageway A45 and a realigned length of navigation which cuts out the old circuitous loop to Higham Ferrers and its notoriously low bridge.

Higham Wharf and the vanished Anchor Inn have been cut off from the navigation too, as well as the adjoining brickworks. The manufacture of bricks and tiles was once prevalent along this stretch of the Nene.

A surprisingly attractive concrete bridge of 1936 carries the A6 across the river at IRTHLINGBOROUGH and contrasts with its 14th century stone predecessor which, being set on a sharp bend, can be difficult to navigate without due care. New moorings have been sited nearby, giving access to Doc Martens shoe factory shop housed in the impressive grandstand of the upwardly mobile local football club, Rushden & Diamonds. Then it's back to the gravel pits and a reach of the river often occupied by canoeists from the local adventure camp.

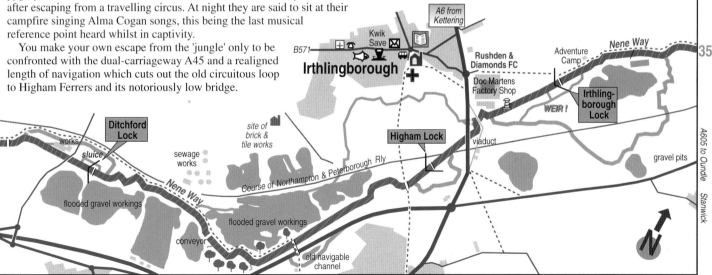

GROWING lovelier by the mile, "The Nen" winds its way past a series of villages with spired churches; Woodford and Denford being the most easily accessible. Flooded gravel workings provide a watery harmony to the river's meanderings, whilst numerous backwaters and weir channels add character to the landscape. Seen from the brows of the valley's low-lying hills, the river reminds one of Constable country; the Suffolk Stour somehow transported to Northamptonshire.

On three occasions the river is crossed by the trackbed of the former Northampton & Peterborough Railway, the bridge spans being still intact and thereby all the more nostalgia-inducing. Opened on 2nd June 1845, the railway served the Nene Valley until its closure - as a result of the Beeching Report - on 2nd May 1964. Its potential as an East-West transport artery has been realised by the A14 trunk road. Ringstead & Addingham station lay out in the wilds, a good walk from either of the villages it was named after. The mill by Lower Ringstead Lock (which has given its name to the local boatyard) was once used for paper making. Kinewell Lake is a nature reserve enjoyed by many species of wildfowl, whilst the adjoining lake is popular with fishermen and stocked with trout and salmon. Pleasant informal moorings are available at Woodford (by the field which slopes down from the church) and Denford (on either bank upstream of the bridge). The Nene Way zig-zags across the valley, there being no continuous riverside path, but the walker thus enjoys more varied perspectives than the boater.

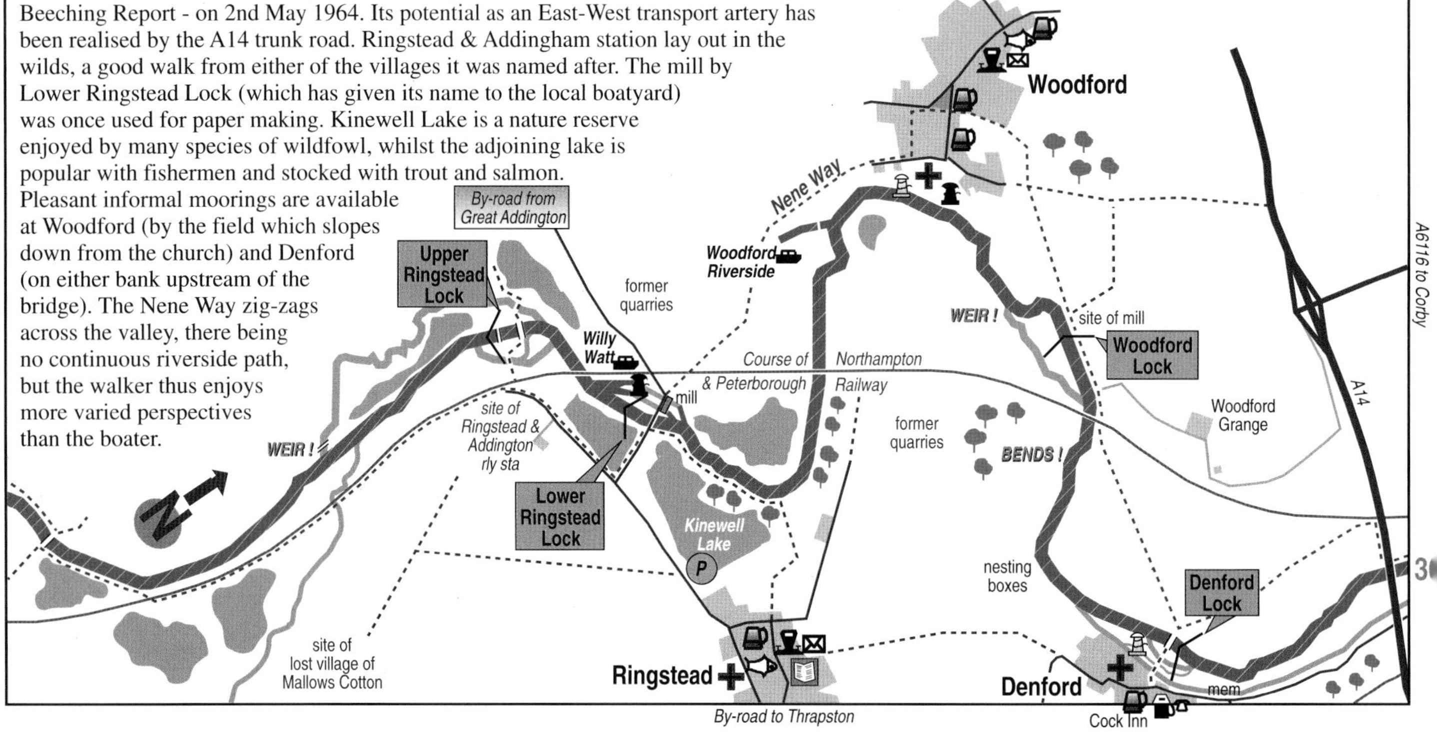

Woodford

Nene Way

Woodford Riverside

By-road from Great Addington

Upper Ringstead Lock

Willy Watt

former quarries

Course of Northampton & Peterborough Railway

WEIR !

site of mill

Woodford Lock

Woodford Grange

A6116 to Corby

A14

mill

site of Ringstead & Addington rly sta

Lower Ringstead Lock

former quarries

BENDS !

Kinewell Lake

P

WEIR !

34

N

nesting boxes

Denford Lock

site of lost village of Mallows Cotton

Ringstead

Denford

Cock Inn

mem

By-road to Thrapston

3

### RINGSTEAD (MAP 35)

Surprisingly workaday village as exemplified by the existence of a number of small factories, council housing, a Co-op and a chip shop. A street name points balefully along a lane to the railway station which no longer exists.

### WOODFORD (MAP 35)

Pleasant, informal moorings on the west bank beneath the church provide access (over a decrepit five-bar gate) to this attractive village grouped about a wide green. Three pubs vie for your patronage and there's a fish & chip shop (closed Sun & Mon) and a well-stocked store. There is also a craft/antique shop.

### DENFORD (MAP 35)

Good moorings and a CAMRA recommended convivial country pub - THE COCK - make Denford a pleasant place to stop, but there is no longer a shop in the village.

T'S here, or hereabouts, that the Nene changes both its name and its nature; evolving from a not exactly hitherto ugly ducking into a beautiful swan, and becoming known in ale houses and general stores bordering its widening valley not so much as "The Nen" as "The Neen".

Three bridges span the river at THRAPSTON, being built of concrete, blue brick and stone in ascending order of age. Naturally the oldest is the most beautiful, its nine segmental arches compressing motor traffic into a traffic light controlled single lane. Approximately eighty feet of overnight mooring space is provided in a backwater by the bridge, an ideal point of disembarkation for Thrapston's fleshpots, but something of test of steering and reversing skills for the steel narrowboat user.

The river slips picturesquely between buildings which look to have once had riverine connections to reach ISLIP LOCK. The adjoining water mill (pictured overleaf) has been attractively restored for residential use. A slightly dull, scrubby landscape bordering flooded gravel pits ensues, but in summer at least you are compensated by the musky scent of balsam and, canallers can still revel in letting their engines rip up to the unaccustomed thrills of seven miles an hour.

Another mill presides over TITCHMARSH LOCK, whose last miller, Alfred Turner, worked here from the begining of the Great War until its closure in the Fifties. He ground the corn, tended the eel-trap and, when the river broke its banks, scrambled to work across a precarious causeway through the orchard.

From Corby

By-road to Oundle

Islip

sewage plant

Islip Mill

Thrapston Bridge

WEIR !

Islip Lock

Bridge Hotel

pipe

Middle Nene Sailing Club

Harper's Brook

Nene Way

All Saints

Dryden House

St Peters

Aldwincle

Wadenhoe

WEIR !

dovecot

mill

Wadenhoe Lock

BENDS !

eyot

Achurch

37

former Neneside Ironworks

MD Marina

Denford

Thrapston

Co-op

Course of Northampton & Peterborough Railway

Course of Kettering & Huntingdon Railway

35

heronry

nature reserve

sluice

P

mill

Brancey Bridge

Middle Nene Cruising Club

Titchmarsh Lock

Roman Road

Thorpe Waterville

A605 to Peterborough

A605 to junction with A14 & A45

During the Second World War he rescued a Canadian airman who'd ditched in the Nene.

The river arcs past Aldwincle (spelt on old maps with a 'k') and its two churches to reach Wadenhoe, by which time it has become as beautiful as any stretch of inland waterway navigation in the country. We found such thoughts agreed with by Denys Watkins Pitchord (alias "BB") in his charming, but long out of print book, "A Summer on the Nene". A belt of trees tumbles down to the river's west bank, whilst, on its not insignificant knoll, St Michael's Norman church (with its interior plaque commemorating local honeymooners murdered by Italian bandits in 1824) cries out to be visited.

A not unpleasant torpor is likely to have descended on boaters. You want to spend your days idling from one reach to another, mooring within easy access of one stone-built and thatched country pub or another. One such pub is the "King's Head", whose gardens spill down to the millstream, whereas the main channel doglegs to the right and passes down through WADENHOE LOCK. Between here and Lilford (Map 37) the Nene is arguably at is supreme loveliest. Everyone will have their own favourite reach but this is indisputably ours, as the navigation twists and bends between water meadows with Wadenhoe Mill and its stream (now a trout fishery) to the north and the low spire of Achurch's 14th century St John the Baptist to the south, the two banks being joined by a rickety timber footbridge which carries the Nene Way footpath.

## WADENHOE (MAP 36)

A small hillside village apparently made in heaven. From the riverbank a street of stone cottages climbs towards the centre where the post office (open Mon, Tue & Thur only) anachronistically advertises itself as a "Postal Telegraph Office". Apparently this was one of the earliest rural telegraph offices in the country, the local landowner being Chancellor during Disraeli's term in office, and relying on close contact with Whitehall from these wilds of Northamptonshire. On a hot August afternoon we trudged up the street to discover a welcome and totally unexpected coolness within the village's beautifully preserved dovecot, still retaining the revolving timber framework by which the dove keeper effected access to the hundreds of pigeon holes.

KINGS HEAD - riverside, customer moorings. Gorgeous country pub with tiled floors (always a good sign) offering Adnams and Marstons beers and mouth-watering food. We lunched on warm baguettes filled with beef and cheese.

Also worth noting is the provision of afternoon teas in the village hall (riverside on the site of the former gasworks!) on summer Sundays.

## ALDWINCLE (MAP 36)

The Nene Way runs through Aldwincle but the river keeps its distance. There are two churches, one with a spire, one with a tower. The latter has not seen a service since 1879. Nearby stands the Old Rectory where Dryden, the poet and playwright, was born in 1631. The village no longer boasts a pub, but its store - H.G. Watts & Son Est 1934 - is as quaint as they come. Calor gas is available from the garage.

## THRAPSTON (MAP 36)

A small town noted for its cattle market - Wednesdays and Fridays are the busy days we were told. St James's parish church contains a stone tablet commemorating a certain John Washington, a forbear of George Washington, first president of the USA. The only other notable building in the town is the old corn exchange with a nicely carved sheaf and plough over its doorway.

BRIDGE HOTEL - They made us very welcome here one enervatingly hot August Sunday and laid on a sumptuous high tea in their comfortable lounge. Thrapston also boasts a Balti, Tandoori, Chinese takeaway, fish & chip shop and homely Charles Wells local called the MASONS ARMS.

The best shop for taking on stores is the Co-op at the far end of the town. There are branches of the Midland, Barclays and Nat West banks. On Tuesdays there's a small street market.

BUSES - Coachlinks service X94 links Thrapston with Wellingborough, Northampton, Oundle and Peterborough. Tel: 01604 702112.

## ISLIP (MAP 36)

Strange how, when communities are divided by a river, one dominates at the other's expense: Buda and Pest; Manchester and Salford; and here, Thrapston and Islip; the latter being effectively nothing more than an elongated village despite the former presence of sizeable ironstone mines in the vicinity. Facilities are limited to two pubs and a post office.

Islip Lock and mill, near Thrapston

**M**EANDERING into middle age, the Nene wanders around the charming market town of Oundle. LOWER BARNWELL LOCK offers the nearest pedestrian access to the town, but there isn't much in the way of suitable moorings. To our mind the best mooring point for visitors lies to the south of NORTH BRIDGE or, alternatively, in the mill stream at Barnwell Mill, though you will need to patronise the restaurant there to avoid mooring fees.

LILFORD LOCK is beautifully located in woodlands called "The Linches". At its tail the Nene is crossed by a graceful, balustraded stone bridge and then the river flows past the grounds of Lilford Hall, a 17th century Jacobean mansion. The Fourth Baron Lilford was a renowned ornithologist responsible for introducing the little owl to these shores in the 1890s.

Flowing in a northerly direction along a wide reach with the villages of Stoke Doyle and Barnwell

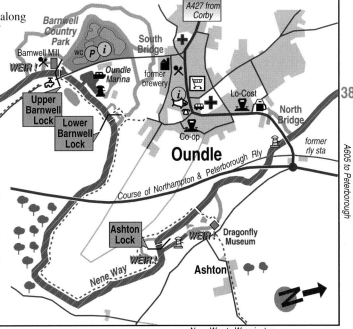

in the middle distance, the Nene arrives at UPPER BARNWELL LOCK, fetchingly overlooked by Barnwell Mill, one of the most handsome watermills on the river, and one of the best eating places too.

Entrance to Oundle Marina can be problematic for lengthy vessels. At LOWER BARNWELL LOCK the local lads were taking advantage of the warm August weather to swim in the Nene when we passed. Curving away from Oundle, the river passes beneath the A605 Thrapston-Peterborough road which backs the trackbed of the old Northampton & Peterborough Railway at this point. See how the old blue brick railway bridge has been harmoniously extended to cope with the extra width required for a two lane road as opposed to a double track railway.

The river really is pretty as it loops round to ASHTON LOCK where good moorings are to be had in the idyllic, tree-flanked surroundings of the mill stream. Here we had the excitement of watching an otter swim across our bows, evidence that these delightful creatures are gaining a toehold in the ecological hierachy of the Nene.

It takes a motorist less than five minutes to drive from Barnwell Mill to North Bridge, but the boater spends the best part of two hours between these points. Yet the soaring, two hundred feet high spire of Oundle's St Peter's parish church is seldom out of sight across the willow-filled watermeadows and we know whose company we'd rather keep.

Oundle's North Bridge bears the dates 1912 and 1571, but its origins as a river crossing go back even further. A backwater stretches up to the former town wharf but it's hardly navigable now. Leaving Oundle astern, there are glimpses of the creamy coloured stone built railway station, closed to most passengers in 1964, but retained - to some locals' chagrin - until 1972 for specials to and from Oundle School which ran at the beginning and end of each term.

## OUNDLE (MAP 37)

Stone built Oundle could melt the stoniest heart, for this is unarguably one of the loveliest, and least spoilt, small towns in England. Much of its atmosphere is derived from the presence of a famous public school at the heart of the town; Sir Peter Scott, the naturalist and early supporter of the Inland Waterways Association was a pupil here. During term-time sudden invasions of young people coincide with breaks between classes, welcome surges of gaiety and insurrection at odds with the usual decorum inherent in Oundle's creamy coloured thoroughfares.

THE MILL - adjacent Upper Barnwell Lock. Excellent restaurant housed in mill conversion, we had a wonderful meal here. Moorings available free of charge if eating. Tel: 01832 272621.

SAN GIORGIO - West Street. Enjoyable Italian restaurant. Good food and friendly welcome Tel: 01832 272723.

THE TALBOT - New Street. Forte Heritage hotel built in 1626 with stone from the ruins of Fotheringhay Castle. Bar and restaurant meals. Tel: 01832 273621.

Lots of other establishments to choose from including: Chinese and Indian restaurants, pubs like "The Angel" and "The Ship" and a really good fish & chip shop (but closed Sundays) in the Market Place.

Shopping is a delightful experience in Oundle where the town's two small supermarkets keep a suitably low profile (LO-COST near Old Bridge, and the CO-OP in St Osyth's Lane). A market is held on Thursdays beside the old Town Hall which dates from 1826. Many individual shops caught our eye and demanded our custom: TRENDALLS delicatessen; AMPS the prize-winning wine merchant; and the SCHOOL BOOKSHOP. Nat West and Barclays have branches in the town.

TOURIST INFORMATION - West Street. Tel: 01832 274333.

BARNWELL COUNTRY PARK - entrance adjacent Oundle Marina. 37 acres of meadowlands and lakes. Visitor Centre & shop. Tel: 01832 273435.

BUSES - Stagecoach/Viscount serices to/from Peterborough. Tel: 01733 54571. Stagecoach United Counties links with Northampton. Tel: 01604 702112.

## ASHTON (MAP 37)

Ashton is famous in conker-playing circles as the venue, each October, for the annual World Conker Championship. The village itself dates from as recently as the beginning of the twentieth century when one of the Rothschilds purchased the local estate and caused a model village to be built. Ahead of its time, Ashton's villagers were blessed with electricity generated at the watermill which is now a centre for the conservation of dragonflies. Does that sound oh so slightly dull? Think again, for we found this to be one of the most delightful small visitor centres we'd encountered anywhere on our inland waterway or scenic railway travellings. Ashton's only sadness lay in the fact that its famous pub, "The Chequered Skipper", named after a now extinct species of butterfly, was now itself extinct (no-one locally could, or would say for how long) following a disastrous fire in its thatched roof.

NATIONAL DRAGONFLY MUSEUM - Ashton Mill. Tel: 01832 272427.

Open weekends only June-September. Museum devoted to the study of dragonflies plus complementary attractions such as blacksmith's forge, thatching, fishing and basket-making displays. Visit includes guided tour of the watermill and its hydro-electric machinery. Tea rooms and shop on site.

## FOTHERINGHAY (MAP 38)

Having known and loved Sandy Denny's beautiful song "Fotheringhay" (off Fairport Convention's "What we did on our Holidays" album) for the best part of thirty years, it was with something of the zest of pilgrims that we made our way by boat to this sweetest and most historic of East Northamptonshire villages. Mooring under the gaze of the church's lantern tower, we "watched the daylight passing" just as Queen Mary does in that plaintive song. As the floodlights came on, we walked up the meadow to the FALCON INN, one of the Nene Valley's most celebrated pubs, recognised in the most recent "Good Pub Guide" as being "Northamptonshire's Dining Pub of the Year". But fate was against us, this being a Monday the chef was off duty and we couldn't even rustle up a sandwich. Consoling ourselves with a glass of Adnams, we returned to the boat and Pot Noodles.

Barnwell Mill, Oundle

CHURCHES with towers predominate at the expense of spires, and none more breathtakingly beautiful than St Mary & All Saints at Fotheringhay. Cattle were drinking from the river and swans gliding by when we turned the corner from Perio and first caught sight of Fotheringhay in all its glory. It would be hard to think of a more exquisite village church in the whole of England and the mind boggles on learning that what remains is perhaps only a third of the size of the original structure.

Perhaps England's prettiest church and perhaps England's prettiest moorings, lie either side of Fotheringhay's four arch, 18th century bridge, well worth the £2 overnight charge collected by the lady at the nearby house who'll also provide you with the morning papers if current affairs

But if Fotheringhay inescapably dominates this section of the river, there is much to admire and fall in love with elsewhere: the watermills at Cotterstock, Perio and Warmington (the latter boarded up and disused); the churches at Cotterstock and Tansor; and the sheer beauty of every reach in the river as it flows through a landscape which is a sort of throwback to a Yeoman England, the equivalent to a Powell-Pressburger cinematic approach - for goodness sake, even the anglers wave!

Between Tansor and Perio a long straight stretch is used by rowers going through their paces. The mill stream at Warmington provides access to the moorings of Elton Boat Club (36ft maximum length). Skirting the wooded perimeter of Elton Park, the river becomes the boundary between Northamptonshire and Cambridgeshire (formerly Huntingdonshire).

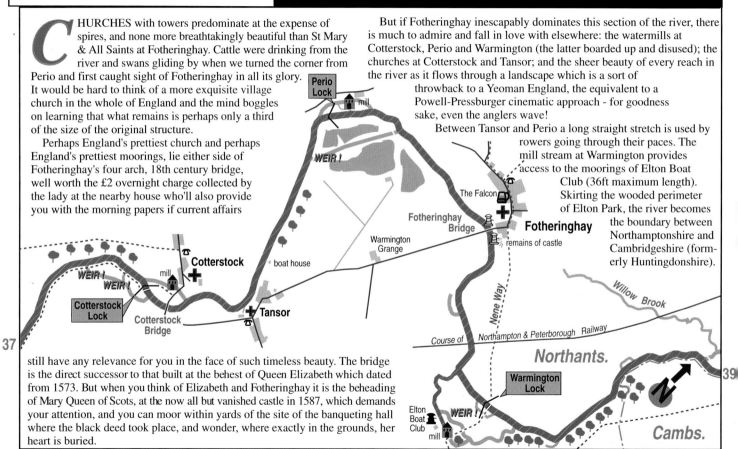

still have any relevance for you in the face of such timeless beauty. The bridge is the direct successor to that built at the behest of Queen Elizabeth which dated from 1573. But when you think of Elizabeth and Fotheringhay it is the beheading of Mary Queen of Scots, at the now all but vanished castle in 1587, which demands your attention, and you can moor within yards of the site of the banqueting hall where the black deed took place, and wonder, where exactly in the grounds, her heart is buried.

Idyllic moorings, Fotheringhay

THE landscape flattens noticeably as the Nene, flowing due north for much of the time between Elton and Wansford, continues its charming progress through the countryside. ELTON LOCK is overlooked by yet another watermill, yet again sadly disused and empty; though the young people in our crew were convinced it contained a ghost. At NASSINGTON a backwater is navigable for small craft as far as moorings provided by the "Queen's Head" pub. Nearby another lost railway encounters the river, the line which once linked Peterborough with Rugby. At the point where this railway and the Northampton line meet, the track remains in place as the western-most extremity of the preserved Nene Valley Railway.

YARWELL LOCK lies at a sharp right-angle to the mill stream. An adjoining caravan park ensures that passage through the lock is rarely achieved without the presence of bystanders.

In the reach between Yarwell and Wansford locks there is evidence, on the east bank, of quarry workings. This represented the Nene's last indigenous commercial trade (indeed the Nene Barge & Lighter Co. are still in business dealing in the sale of sand and aggregates by road!) in the shape of locally quarried stone carried downstream by motor barge for reinforcing the Nene's banks along its tidal stretch beyond Peterborough. Here too were laid up some of the last wooden Fen Lighters so characteristic of trade on the Nene. Generally about forty feet long and capable of carrying twenty tons of cargo, they were often worked in 'trains' or 'gangs'.

WANSFORD often comes with the sobriquet "in England". The story goes that a local rustic had fallen asleep in a haystack (or haycock) and been borne downstream by a flash flood. Awaking just as he passed beneath Wansford Bridge, he asked his whereabouts, and on being told that

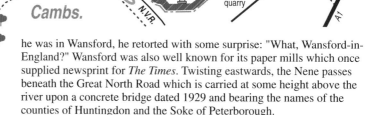

he was in Wansford, he retorted with some surprise: "What, Wansford-in-England?" Wansford was also well known for its paper mills which once supplied newsprint for *The Times*. Twisting eastwards, the Nene passes beneath the Great North Road which is carried at some height above the river upon a concrete bridge dated 1929 and bearing the names of the counties of Huntingdon and the Soke of Peterborough.

## ELTON (MAP 39)

An apparently thriving village (with its own well produced magazine) in Fitzwilliam Hunt territory and, being on the eastern bank of the river, located in Cambridgeshire. The large hall (open to the public on Wed & Sun afternoons in July & August) and its extensive parkland lie away from the river in the vicinity of the A605 Oundle-Peterborough main road.

THE CROWN - delightful stone and thatch country pub highly regarded for its bar and restaurant meals (though not on Sunday or Monday evenings!).
LOCH FYNE OYSTER BAR - adjacent to A605, 10 minutes walk from Elton Lock. Open all day from 9am for breakfasts, lunches and dinners. Tel: 01832 280298.

VILLAGE STORES - Middle Street. Open daily for groceries, papers and post office facilities.

BUSES - Viscount services to/from Oundle and Peterborough. Tel: 01733 54571.

## NASSINGTON (MAP 39)

Large U shaped village on the west bank of the Nene notable in that King Canute stayed here on one of his tours.

QUEENS HEAD - customer moorings on back water (length limitations!). Comfortable country pub offering food and accommodation.
BLACK HORSE - 17th century inn famous for miles for its food!

A general store, butcher and wine merchant provide an unexpectedly wide range of facilities for a village of this size.

PREBENDAL MANOR HOUSE - open Weds, Suns & Bank Hol Mons 2-5.30 May-September. Tel: 01780 782575. Northamptonshire's oldest manor house built for the Prebend of Lincoln Cathedral with parts dating from as early as the 13th century. Other attractions include a dovecot (one of three we came upon in the Nene Valley), tithe barn and medieval garden with fish ponds. Teas.

BUSES - Viscount services to/from Oundle and Peterborough. Tel: 01733 54571.

## WANSFORD (MAP 39)

Quaint stone cottages with dormer windows caressed by some of the highest hollyhocks you've ever seen characterise Wansford, now a sleepy backwater since the Great North Road was diverted away from the old bridge in 1929.

THE HAYCOCK - former coaching inn now an exceptionally comfortable hotel. Facilities for non-residents include a formal dining room and a less formal eating area. River travellers such as ourselves are made to feel welcome in the latter and here, it has to be said, we enjoyed one of the best meals of our lives in pristine

surroundings with an attentive staff. Even the children behaved immaculately. We came out afterwards, through the walled garden, past locals engaged in the serious business of petanque, at the end of a dream like evening, returning to our boat moored at the foot of the hotel's spacious grounds. Tel: 01780 782223.
THE PAPER MILLS - village centre. Attractive local offering excellent choice of food.

ROD VERNUMS - village stores, post office and newsagency. Other shops in Wansford include outlets for oriental pottery, antiques, shoes, ladies clothes and ornamental lighting.

NENE VALLEY RAILWAY - Wansford Station (Map 40). Tel: 01780 784440/4. Preserved steam line running between Yarwell (no station), Wansford and Peterborough. Operational at weekends in spring and autumn and most weekdays in the summer. Shop and cafe at Wansford station - informal moorings to north-west of railway bridge.

BUSES - Viscount services to/from Peterborough. Tel: 01780 54571.

## PETERBOROUGH (MAP 41)

Surprisingly small and homely, Peterborough is basically a small cathedral town which has burgeoned on the back of successive industrial revolutions to its present city status. Its outskirts remind you of nothing so much as Milton Keynes, but in the centre evidence of a much older provenance remains engagingly and entertainingly apparent. The cathedral, containing the tomb of Queen Katherine of Aragon, is most impressive, though these days they ask you to pay to go in. One or two old thoroughfares remain, such as Priestgate, but elsewhere the general effect is stridently modernistic.

CHARTERS - converted Dutch barge moored upstream of Town Bridge. Lunches and wide choice of real ales.
THE GRAIN BARGE - Chinese restaurant moored downstream of Town Bridge.
THE BOATHOUSE - Greene King, family friendly 'all dayer' located on mooring-friendly backwater near The Boardwalks.

Good range of shops within easy reach of the riverbank. Bridge Street is the main thoroughfare, creating a pleasant traffic-free link with Queensgate's covered shopping centre. ASDA have a supermarket in the Rivergate Shopping Centre.

BUSES - services throughout the local area from Queensgate bus station.
TRAINS - major railhead on East Coast Main Line, plus local and cross-country services. Tel: 0345 484950.

TOURIST INFORMATION - Bridge Street. Tel: 01733 317336.

**P**OSSIBLY conscious of the impending approach of Peterborough, the Nene seems to reprise all the beauty that downstreamers have come to know and love. Old maps indicate the presence of fords (one of them known poetically as 'Flaxen Ford') in the neighbourhood of Stibbington. An intriguing obelisk stands on the river's south bank. We tried to get ashore to see if there was any inscription on it but were defeated by an abundance of August nettles. Sorry! The river parallels the trackbed of the relatively short-lived Wansford & Stamford railway. Nicknamed the "bread and onion line", it was closed in 1931. Across the river from Wansford station it formed a junction with the lines from Peterborough to Rugby and Northampton now incorporated in the preserved Nene Valley Railway, famous amongst enthusiasts and film-makers (looking for a little foreign colour) for its collection of European locomotives and rolling stock. When we passed they were steaming a handsome Swedish 4-6-0.

The watermill at WATER NEWTON is delightful, likewise Castor. Between them the Nene curves enchantingly past the site of the Roman town of Durobrivae which lay astride Ermine Street, the Roman road linking London with Lincoln and York. Our 1901 six inch reference map depicts the river meandering elaborately in the vicinity of Castor. Nowadays this channel has become a reed-fringed oxbow shaded by willows. As well as a watermill, Castor also had a windmill, whose derelict bricktower is still more or less intact. Nene Way travellers pass close to it, boaters view it from across the watermeadows.

Peterborough Cruising Club have extensive moorings upstream of ALWALTON LOCK beyond which the river curves northwards again and passes beneath the Nene Valley Railway. MILTON FERRY BRIDGE dates from early in the 18th century having taken the place of a ferry which once operated at this point.

**A** municipal air descends upon the river, though it remains discernibly rural in nature until you reach ORTON LOCK and its adjoining sluices, which can generate a strong cross-current and require due care and attention. By Bluebell Bridge, a branch gives access to OVERTON LAKE where moorings are available for visiting boaters, a useful alternative to 'downtown' Peterborough. In the summer months you could moor here and journey into the city centre aboard one of the Nene Valley Railway's steam trains. Another mooring option can be taken up in the backwater adjoining "The Boathouse" restaurant/pub, but one imagines that most boaters will want to complete their journey and moor in the city itself at the Town Quay, just downstream of the Custom House.

But we're rushing ahead of ourselves and missing such detail as the metal screens at Thorpe Wood Golf Course erected to protect passing boaters and pedestrians from mis-directed tee shots. Likewise we've not yet mentioned Peterborough Yacht Club's extensive linear moorings where many cabin cruisers are accompanied by their own timber chalet.

Your first glimpse of Peterborough's cathedral is likely to be framed by electricity pylons. A succession of railway bridges, the last and best of them a cast iron structure by Cubitt and Brassey dated 1850, precedes the river's passage through the city centre. Modern flats (ironically not unlike those at Northampton) dominate the north bank in a bland sort of way, but it's Peterborough (Town) Bridge and the Old Custom House which combine to provide a much needed sense of identity at this point. Downstream lies Peterborough's own "Embankment" and pleasantly secure moorings with water, rubbish and Elsan disposal facilities on hand. East of here you can proceed (though not with Pearson's help unfortunately) to the tidal Nene at Dog-in-a-Doublet or the Middle Level via Stanground Sluice. Good luck - if only we could come with you!

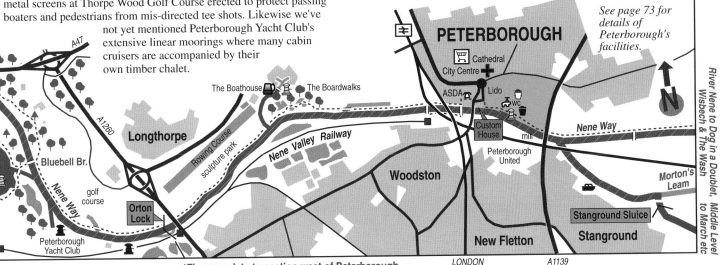

*See page 73 for details of Peterborough's facilities.*

*Figures relate to section west of Peterborough.*

## Hire Bases

|  |  |  |
|---|---|---|
| ALVECHURCH BOAT CENTRES - Gayton Marina, River Nene, Maps 19/30. Tel: 0121 445 2909. | One of four bases. | Book direct. |
| AYNHO WHARF - Aynho Wharf, Oxford Canal, Map 12. Tel: 01869 338483. | Day boats only. | Book direct. |
| BLACK PRINCE - Napton Marina, Oxford Canal, Map 7. Tel: 01527 575115. | | Book direct. |
| BLISWORTH TUNNEL BOATS - Blisworth, Grand Union Canal, Map 20. Tel: 01604 858868. | Day boat hire. | Book direct. |
| BRAUNSTON BOATS - Braunston, Grand Union Canal, Map 6. Tel: 01788 891079. | | Book direct. |
| BRIDGEWATER BOATS - Berkhamsted, Grand Union Canal, Map 28A. Tel: 01442 863615. | | Book direct. |
| CANALBOAT HOLIDAYS - Weedon, Grand Union Canal, Map 18. Tel: 01327 340739. | | Book direct. |
| CLIFTON CRUISERS - Clifton Wharf, Oxford Canal, Map 4. Tel: 01788 543570. | | Hoseasons 01502 501010. |
| CLUB LINE CRUISERS - Swan Lane Wharf, Coventry, Map 1. Tel: 024 7625 8864. | | Blakes 01603 782911. |
| COLLEGE CRUISERS - Combe Road, Oxford, Map 16. Tel: 01865 554343. | Day boat hire. | Hoseasons 01502 501010. |
| GREBE CANAL CRUISES - Pitstone Wharf, Grand Union Canal, Map 27. Tel: 01296 661920. | Day boats only. | Book direct. |
| MILTON KEYNES MARINA - Milton Keynes, Grand Union Canal, Map 23. Tel: 01908 672672. | Day boats only. | Book direct. |
| NAPTON NARROWBOATS - Napton, Oxford Canal, Map 7. Tel: 01926 813644. | | Hoseasons 01502 501010. |
| OXFORDSHIRE NARROWBOATS - Lower Heyford, Oxford Canal, Map 13. Tel: 01869 340348. | Day boat hire. | Hoseasons 01502 501010. |
| ROSE NARROWBOATS - Stretton-under-Fosse, Oxford Canal, Map 2. Tel: 01788 832449. | | Book direct. |
| SOVEREIGN NARROWBOATS - Banbury, Oxford Canal, Map 10. Tel: 01295 275657. | | Book direct. |
| UNION CANAL CARRIERS - Braunston, Grand Union Canal, Map 6. Tel: 01788 890784. | | Blakes 01603 782911. |
| WELTONFIELD NARROWBOATS - Welton, Grand Union Canal, Map 17. Tel: 01327 842282. | | Book direct. |
| WILLOW WREN - Rugby, Oxford Canal, Map 4. Tel: 01788 562183. | | Book direct. |
| WYVERN SHIPPING - Linslade, Grand Union Canal, Map 26. Tel: 01525 372355. | | Book direct. |
| VIKING AFLOAT - Rugby, Oxford Canal, Map 4. Tel: 01905 610660. | One of four bases. | Book direct. |

# Boatyards

AYNHO WHARF - Aynho, Oxford Canal, Map 12. Tel: 01869 338483.

BAXTER BOATFITTING - Yardley Gobion, Grand Union Canal, Map 21. Tel: 01908 542844.

BILLING AQUADROME - Billing, River Nene, Map 31. Tel: 01604 408181.

BRAUNSTON MARINA - Braunston, Grand Union Canal, Map 6. Tel: 01788 891373.

COWROAST MARINA - Tring, Grand Union Canal, Map 28A. Tel: 01442 823222.

FENNY MARINA - Fenny Compton, Oxford Canal, Map 8. Tel: 01295 770461.

GREBE CANAL CRUISES - Pitstone Wharf, Grand Union Canal, Map 27. Tel: 01296 661920.

MILL MARINA - Thrapston, River Nene, Map 36. Tel: 01832 732850.

MILTON KEYNES MARINA - Milton Keynes, Map 23. Tel: 01908 672672.

MORSE MARINE - Tooleys Boatyard, Banbury, Oxford Canal, Map 10. Tel: 01925 261221.

OUNDLE MARINA - Oundle, River Nene, Map 37. Tel: 01832 272762.

STIBBINGTON BOATYARD - Stibbington, River Nene, Map 40. Tel: 01780 783144.

STOWE HILL MARINE/MILLAR MARINE - Stowe Hill Wharf, Grand Union Canal, Map 18. Tel: 01327 341365.

WATERWAYS SERVICES - Nether Hayford, Grand Union Canal, Map 18. Tel: 01327 342300.

WHILTON MARINA - Whilton Locks, Grand Union Canal, Map 17. Tel: 01327 842577.

WILLOWBRIDGE MARINA - Stoke Hammond, Grand Union Canal, Map 24. Tel: 01908 643242.

WILLY WATT - Ringstead, River Nene, Map 35. Tel: 01933 622038.

WOODFORD RIVERSIDE - Woodford, River Nene, Map 35. Tel: 01832 734501.

KEN YATES MARINE - Billing, River Nene, Map 31. Tel: 01604 408312.

**Information 1**

## How to use the Maps

There are forty-two numbered maps whose layout is shown by the Route Planner inside the front cover. Maps 1 to 16 cover the Oxford Canal between Hawkesbury, on the outskirts of Coventry, and Oxford where there is a link to the Thames. Maps 17 to 29 cover the Grand Union Canal between Braunston and Berkhamsted (Map 28A) and Aylesbury. Maps 30 to 41 cover the Northampton Arm and River Nene between Gayton and Peterborough. The maps are easily read in either direction. The simplest way of progressing from map to map is to proceed to the next map numbered from the edge of the map you are on. Figures quoted at the top of each map refer to distance per map, locks per map and average cruising time. An alternative indication of timings from centre to centre can be found on the Route Planner. Obviously, cruising times vary with the nature of your boat and the number of crew at your disposal, so quoted times should be taken only as an estimate. Neither do times quoted take into account any delays which might occur at lock flights in high season.

## Using the Text

Each map is accompanied by a route commentary. Details of settlements passed through are given together with itemised or summarised information on facilities. Regular readers will already be familiar with our somewhat irreverent approach. But we 'tell it as we find it', in the belief that the users of this guide will find this attitude more valuable than a strict towing of the tourist publicity line.

## Towpath Walking

The simplest way to go canal exploring is on foot. It costs largely nothing and you are free to concentrate on the passing scene; something that boaters are not always at liberty to do. Both the Oxford and Grand Union canals are now recognised as long distance footpaths in their own right, as is the Nene Way, so that all the waterways covered in this particular Canal Companion are accompanied by paths given formal status, auguring well for their upkeep. As usual the maps show the quality of the towpath, and whilst it does vary from area to area, none of it should prove problematical for anyone innured to the vicissitudes of country walking. We recommend the use of public transport to facilitate 'one-way' itineraries but stress the advisability of checking up to date details on the telephone numbers quoted.

## Towpath Cycling

Cycling canal towpaths is an increasingly popular activity, but one which British Waterways - the still quaintly nationalised body responsible for the upkeep of the bulk of Britain's navigable inland waterways - is only slowly coming to terms with. At present it is necessary for cyclists wishing to use towpaths to acquire a free of charge permit from a British Waterways office - see opposite.

## Boating

Boating on inland waterways is an established, though relatively small, facet of the UK holiday industry. There are over 20,000 privately owned boats registered on the canals, but in addition to these numerous firms offer boats for hire. These range from small operators with half a dozen boats to sizeable fleets run by companies with several bases.

Most hire craft have all the creature comforts you are likely to expect. In the excitement of planning a boating holiday you may give scant thought to the contents of your hire boat, but at the end of a hard day's boating such matters take on more significance, and a well equipped, comfortable boat, large enough to accommodate your crew with something to spare, can make the difference between a good holiday and an indifferent one.

Traditionally, hire boats are booked out by the week or fortnight, though many firms now offer more flexible short breaks or extended weeks. All reputable hire firms give newcomers tuition in boat handling and lock working, and first-timers soon find themselves adapting to the pace of things 'on the cut'.

## Navigational Advice

LOCKS are part of the charm of canal cruising, but they are potentially dangerous environments for children, pets and careless adults. Use of them should be methodical and unhurried, whilst special care should be exercised in rain, frost and snow when slippery hazards abound. We lack space for detailed instructions on lock operation: trusting that if you own your own boat you will, by definition, already be experienced in canal cruising; whilst first-time hire boaters should be given tuition in the operation of locks before they set out.

On the OXFORD CANAL the locks are of the standard narrow variety but on the GRAND UNION (except for the Northampton and Aylesbury arms) and the RIVER NENE the locks are widebeam and capable of accepting two narrowboats side by side. On the Grand Union Canal, bedevilled by water shortages in recent summers, British Waterways encourage the sharing of locks to save water. This is obviously rarely a problem on the Nene, but here sharing of the locks means sharing of the work and can thus be most welcome. Turbulence can be a problem when travelling uphill in wide locks, especially if your boat is the only vessel in the lock at the time. A rope cast around the lockside bollards will usually solve this. You might also benefit from opening the paddle on the same side as your boat first, this tends to hold the boat against the lock wall and prevent it from crashing about as the water floods in.

LIFT BRIDGES are a feature of the OXFORD CANAL but the majority of them remain open to boats except when being used by local farmers to gain access to their fields on the far bank. The moral is to 'leave them as you find them' - the bridges, that is, not the farmers.

MOORING on the canals featured in this guide is per usual practice - ie on the towpath side, away from sharp bends, bridge-holes and narrows. An 'open' bollard symbol represents visitor mooring sites; either as designated specifically by British Waterways or, in some cases, as recommended by our personal experience. Of course, one of the great joys of canal boating has always been the ability to moor wherever (sensibly) you like. In recent years, however, it has become obvious, particularly in urban areas, that there are an increasing number of undesirable locations where mooring is not to be recommended for fear of vandalism, theft or abuse. It would be nice if local authorities would be prepared to provide pleasant, secure, overnight facilities for passing boaters who, after all, bring the commerce of tourism in their wake.

CLOSURES (or 'stoppages' in canal parlance) traditionally occur on the inland waterways between November and April, during which time most of the heavy maintenance work is undertaken. Occasionally, however, an emergency stoppage, or perhaps water restriction, may be imposed at short notice, closing part of the route you intend to use. Up to date details are usually available from hire bases. Alternatively, British Waterways provide a recorded message for private boaters on 01923 201402. Stoppages are also listed on BW's web site at http://www.british-waterways.org

## Emergencies

British Waterways operate a central emergency telephone service. Dial the operator and ask for FREEPHONE CANALS. For mobile users the number is 01384 215785.

## Useful Contacts

BRITISH WATERWAYS - Oxford & Grand Union Canals, The Stop House, Braunston, Northants NN11 7JQ. Tel: 01788 890666. Fax: 01788 890222. Grand Union Canal (south of Stowe Hill - Map 18), Marsworth Junction, Tring, Herts HP23 4LZ. Tel: 01442 825938. Fax: 01442 890648.
ENVIRONMENT AGENCY (RIVER NENE) - Kingfisher House, Goldhay Way, Orton Goldhay, Peterborough PE2 5ZR. Tel: 01733 371811.
ENVIRONMENT AGENCY (RIVER THAMES) - Kings Meadow Road, Reading RG1 8DQ. Tel: 01734 535000.

## Societies

The Inland Waterways Association was founded in 1946 to campaign for retention of the canal system. Many routes now open to pleasure boaters may not have been so but for this organisation. Membership details may be obtained from: Inland Waterways Association, PO Box 114, Rickmansworth WD3 1ZY. Tel: 01923 711114. Fax: 01923 897000.

## Web Sites

George's Canal Boating: www.canals.com
British Waterways: www.british-waterways.org
Environment Agency: www.environment-agency.gov.uk
Pearsons Canal Companions: www.jmpearson.co.uk

## Acknowledgements

Thanks: to Brian Collings for the signwritten cover; to Toby, Jackie & Karen for updates; and to Steve Webb and all at Lithomaster for production.

# Waterways World

## the *NUMBER ONE* inland waterway magazine

- **news** each month *Waterways World* reports all that is happening around the waterway system
- **canal heritage** restoration reports, waterway history - the boats, people and companies that worked and built the canal system ● **boat sales** more boats for sale every month than any other inland waterway magazine

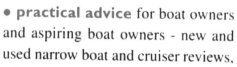

● **practical advice** for boat owners and aspiring boat owners - new and used narrow boat and cruiser reviews, engine developments, the latest equipment, and much more ● **enjoyment of the waterways** explore a different waterway each month with cruising reports, waterside walks, hire boat reviews, continental cruising

●

**Available from newsagents, boatyards and on subscription**

Published by Waterways World Ltd. The Well House. High Street. Burton-on-Trent. Staffordshire DE14 1JQ.  Telephone 01283 742970